DRESSMAKING METHOD IN DETAIL

DRESSMAKING
Method
in
Detail
Wendy Gibson

The Book Guild Ltd
Sussex, England

———

The Book Guild Limited
Temple House
25 High Street
Lewes, Sussex

First published 1987
© Wendy Gibson 1987

Set in Linotron Bembo

Typesetting by Book Economy Services

Printed in Great Britain by
Unwin Brothers
Woking, Surrey

ISBN 0 86332 223 9

CONTENTS

Introduction

Needlecraft is a most useful craft but it should also be enjoyable providing the worker with a sense of satisfaction in producing well made and attractive garments and articles. To be able to do this it is essential to learn how to use the tools of the trade correctly and to learn the basic elements of the craft very thoroughly. With continued practice in the methods of garment construction the worker will also gain speed as well as skill. Quick methods are an obvious advantage but the worker should beware of skipping the early stages of preparation, which are an essential of any craft, as this can so easily lead to sloppy working and a poor finished result.

Some styles are very much easier to make than others and it is a good idea to start on such a style. This is particularly true for a young person as they could become discouraged with their progress if they become entangled in a difficult style. Success in simple things leads to success in more difficult things. Commercial producers of paper patterns are well aware of this and to help the novice these easy styles are often labelled 'Simple to Sew'.

As with patterns so with fabrics. Some fabrics are so slippery or difficult in some other way, eg pattern on fabric needs to be matched, that they are not suitable for a novice. It is better to choose a firmly woven fabric such as cotton or cotton/polyester for a first attempt.

The knowledge that is learnt as one progresses in the craft is extremely useful when buying clothes. Usually it is cheaper to make than buy but this must be weighed against the time it takes to make, the finished result, the pleasure of making and the quality of fabric one can buy. When deciding to buy, rather than make, dressmaking knowledge will help one to judge the quality of fabric and workmanship in the garment being considered to see if value for money is being obtained.

The reader is taken step by step through the various processes in different aspects of the craft and it is hoped that this book will provide a sound foundation in the craft.

1

EQUIPMENT

When considering equipment to use, many of the items mentioned are already in the home. Some will, of course, have to be bought by the 'first timers' but it should be remembered that a few tools of good quality which are well looked after are better than many of inferior quality. Young people learning the craft in schools are lucky indeed to have the use of a wide variety of up to date tools and aids to the craft before they need to purchase their own.

EQUIPMENT WHICH IS USUALLY IN THE HOME

1. Table

This should be situated where there is ample light and should be of a comfortable height. Very often the dining table is used and if this has a highly polished surface, it should be covered with a protective cloth of some sort to prevent pins and scissors scratching the surface.

2. Iron

Most irons are now thermostatically controlled for use on different fabrics. Many homes have a steam iron and although this is useful for dressmaking it is by no means essential.

3. Pressing Cloth

This can be used wet or dry according to the material being pressed. It needs to be of a firmly woven, lint free cloth such as old cotton sheeting or firm muslin.

4   Ironing Board/Table

This should be covered by a thin blanket or similar fabric and then by a clean lint free cloth. For dressmaking, a better result is obtained if work is pressed on a firm board or old fashioned table while the reverse is true when pressing traditional embroideries.

5.   Storage Space

A cupboard or drawer where work may be kept when not being worked on, will keep it clean and fresh and avoid small bits getting lost. Each individual will arrange this to suit the convenience of the household.

6.   A long Mirror

This is very useful when trying on partly made garments to see if they fit correctly. Nowadays many wardrobes have such a mirror and there is no need to buy one specially.

EQUIPMENT FOR THE WORKBOX

This small equipment is best kept together in some sort of container, which need not be an expensive specially made workbox.

   These items of equipment marked ★ are considered necessary: the other items can be purchased as and when needed.

1.   Scissors

It is particularly important that these should be of good quality metal so that they may be re-sharpened from time to time. Avoid letting them be used for all sorts of jobs round the house. It is a good idea to keep an old pair in the workbox for trimming paper.

★ Cutting Out Scissors

These need to be at least 20 cms long for use on thin and medium fabrics and longer for thick fabrics. Tailors' shears are not mis-named as they are very large indeed and not really suitable for use on finer fabrics.

   Whatever the length of scissors you choose the handles should be shaped for comfort, i.e. one side will have a round thumb hole and the other side a longer hole to take three fingers. If you are left handed there are special scissors designed for you.

The longer the scissors the heavier they will be and if the extra weight is likely to be a problem, as with very young or older workers with arthritic tendencies, it is well worth while searching for one of the lighter weight type which are now on the market.

★Small Scissors – about 10 cms long

These are for snipping cottons and trimming seam allowances etc. They do need to be sharp at the point of the blade.

Embroidery Scissors – about 6 cms long

These are only needed for very fine embroidery and should have fine sharp points.

Pinking Shears

These tend to be expensive but can be useful for cutting out fabrics which fray very quickly. The pinked edge will stop the turnings fraying too badly while the garment is being made. It is better not to regard pinking as a final method of neatening except perhaps on non-fraying materials such as felt. For those interested in examination work, pinking is generally not accepted on garments.

2. Needles

The size and shape of the needle to be used depends on the worker and the purpose for which it is to be used.

★Sharpes are used for most general purposes. They vary slightly in length and have an oval eye.

Betweens are considerably shorter than Sharpes and have a bevelled eye. The experienced worker can work much more quickly and finely with this size needle.

Crewel or Embroidery Needles are similar in length to Sharpes but have a longer eye to take the thicker threads used in embroidery. They can be used for tacking as they are quicker to thread than Sharpes.

★ ★ ★ ★

These three types of needles are available in sizes 1-10, the smaller the number the thicker the needle. The most useful sizes are 6, 7, 8 and 9 and it is possible to buy these sizes in assorted packets.

★ ★ ★ ★

Specialised Needles

Darners are similar to Crewel but much longer. They are sold in sizes 1-8 (thick to fine).

Beading Needles are similar to Darners but very much finer. They are used for sewing fine beads onto garments or embroidery. They can be difficult to thread for those who have to wear spectacles but a No.10 Sharpes makes a good substitute.

Bodkins are thick needles with a blunted end and are useful for threading ribbons and cords etc.

Chenille Needles are similar in appearance to Crewel needles but are much thicker to take Chenille wool and other thick threads which are used in modern embroidery. Sizes are from 16 (thick) to 24 (fine).

Tapestry Needles are similar to Chenille needles but have a blunted end so that the needle passes easily between the threads of canvas or evenly woven fabric which is used for counted thread embroidery. Sizes are from 13 (thick) to 24 (fine).

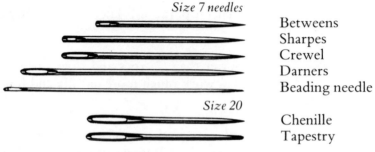

Size 7 needles

Betweens
Sharpes
Crewel
Darners
Beading needle

Size 20

Chenille
Tapestry

Comparative lengths of needles of same size.

3.   Pins

★Steel pins 2.5 cms long should be used for general purposes. Good quality steel pins are packed with a small square of special paper which will absorb moisture and stop the pins going rusty and then marking the fabric.

Lillikins are fine pins 1.3 cms long and are for use on very fine fabrics.

Glass headed pins are about 3.0 cms long and are useful for holding several layers of fabric in position as in pleats or hems.

4.   Tape Measure

★A good quality, non fraying and non stretch material such as fibre-glass should be used for this. It should be marked on both sides and until the transition to metric measures is complete, it is useful if this marking is in both inches and centimetres.

5.   Threads

★For thread marking and tacking use white or coloured tacking thread according to colour of material. Tacking thread is cheaper and softer than sewing thread.

For Permanent stitching use Sylko, Drima, Gutterman pure silk, sewing cotton according to colour and fibre content of material. These are usually purchased with material to ensure a good match. Most good needlewomen will also keep black and white sewing thread in their workbox.

6.   Thimble

It is now accepted that good fine sewing can be done without a thimble. If one is used it should be worn on the middle finger of the working hand. A steel lined one, although heavier to wear, will last much longer than a plastic one.

7.   Tailors Chalk is sold in triangular shaped pieces with sharpened edges and can be had in several colours. It is useful for transferring some markings from paper pattern to material. It will brush off fabric fairly easily when used lightly.

8.   Carbon Paper is special carbon paper for use in dressmaking and

is available in several colours. It does not brush off and therefore must be used on wrong side of material. It washes off fairly easily.

9.   **Stillettos** have a round shaft with a pointed end, often mounted on a convenient handle, and are used mainly for making eyelets.

10.   **Other useful items of equipment**

Skirt Marker. This is a measuring stick mounted on a small base to hold the stick vertical and is a useful aid to getting a skirt hem level. Some models have a puffer can of white powder attached but this is not essential.

Sleeve Board. This is a small version of an ironing board which makes pressing sleeves and intricate parts of a garment much easier.

Tailors Ham. This is a slightly rounded, egg-shaped pad which is useful for pressing curved seams and other shaped parts.

All the equipment mentioned so far has been considered mainly from the view point of hand sewing. However, if any amount of dressmaking is to be done it is essential to have the use of a machine. While it is perhaps convenient to borrow one occasionally, once the worker becomes more proficient the purchase of a machine may be considered.

CHOICE OF SEWING MACHINE

Cost

There are so many sewing machines on the market nowadays that it is essential to understand of what each type is capable. There are machines which will do almost all types of stitches down to those which do only a basic straight stitch. The more complicated the machine, the more it will cost and this must be considered when making a choice. It is simply not worth paying for advanced techniques if one is never likely to use them. One must ask oneself what can be afforded and exactly what is expected of the machine.

Types of Machine

Many people think of an automatic machine as one on which they do not have to turn a handle. This is not so. There are four main categories of machine:

(1)   Straight stitch only
(2)   Swing needle (zigzag)
(3)   Semi automatic
(4)   Fully automatic

(1)   Straight stitch machines may be hand machines or powered by treadle or electricity. The obvious advantage of the latter are that they are quicker and less tiring to use and they leave both hands free to guide the work.

Most of the machines which just do straight stitch also have a reversing mechanism which can be a quick method of securing the end of machining. Included in the price it is usual to have several attachments, the most useful being a zipper foot.

These machines, although the cheapest, have a fairly limited application and unless economy is the prime factor it is perhaps better to consider choosing a swing needle machine.

(2)   Swing needle machines. The most unsophisticated of these incorporate all the facilities of the straight stitchers with an adjustable width zigzag stitch. At its closest, zigzag stitch will make very serviceable buttonholes and at other widths will finish seams so they do not fray.

Twin needles can often be bought as an extra and are useful for tucking or for double lines of top stitching.

(3)   Semi automatic machines include all the features of the basic swing needle machines as well as several extra features that add finish to work on difficult fabrics.

The most important of these are the stretch stitches for use on stretch fabrics such as jersey fabrics. Multi stitch zigzag or straight stretch will give a seam that really expands with body movement.

Usually a selector is available for a blind hemming stitch which gives an almost invisible hem finish when used correctly.

Buttonholes are usually easier on semi-automatic machines as the material does not have to be turned.

There is a useful range of attachments supplied and there is often a small range of embroidery stitches.

(4)   Fully automatic machines provide the same range of practical stitches as a semi automatic but a much larger range of decorative stitches. Many incorporate an over-locking stitch which is similar to that produced by an industrial machine.

Where a fully automatic machine scores is that the worker does much less. Some machines require that you put in a special cam, while others have a range of selector dials which set the internal programme going. The worker merely guides the material.

These machines are much the most expensive and one must be sure that the extra cost is justified by the amount of sewing to be done.

Other considerations affecting choice

(i)   If the machine has to be stored in a confined space when not in use, is it:-

(a)   easy to pack into its case?
(b)   easy to lift?

(ii)   If for various reasons, the machine must be carried about is it:-

(a)   really portable?
(b)   does it still do all the stitches that are required?

(iii)   If cost is a prime factor, would it be better to have a good reconditioned second-hand machine with a guarantee?

(iv)   Is there a reliable maintenance service available locally for the make under consideration and are spare parts easily obtainable?

Learning to use the machine

Acquiring this skill early can save hours of frustration later on.

Identify the parts of the machine

These will vary slightly from machine to machine as will their relative positions. The instruction booklet provided with each machine will have a clear diagram of the various parts, but the following diagram shows the main parts for a free arm zigzag machine.

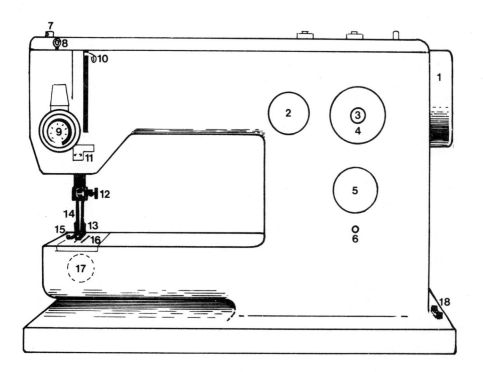

Main parts of a free arm zigzag sewing machine

(1)	Balance wheel	(10)	Take up lever
(2)	Needle position knob	(11)	Thread guide
(3)	Reverse feed knob	(12)	Needle clamp screw
(4)	Stitch length regulator	(13)	Presser bar
(5)	Stitch width regulator	(14)	Needle
(6)	Drop feed knob	(15)	Presser foot
(7)	Thread guide	(16)	Feed dog in throat plate
(8)	Thread guide	(17)	Spool in spool case compartment
(9)	Upper thread tension knob	(18)	Power on/off switch

Learn to thread the machine

Unless the machine is properly threaded with correct tension on both upper and lower threads the machine will not stitch properly. Detailed instructions for both winding the spool and threading the machine are found in the instruction booklet. It is a good idea to memorise the details of the machine you are likely to use as this will save much time.

If one is faced with a strange machine and no instruction booklet (they do get lost) the following three points will help to thread the machine correctly.

1)   The spool must be wound evenly before it is placed in the spool case, which may be removable or set in the base of the machine close to the needle. Check to see that the thread from the spool passes between a springy piece of metal and the spool case.

2)   The upper thread usually follows a basic pattern:-

> Cotton reel holder
> Thread guide
> Tension guide and spring
> 2 or 3 thread guides
> Needle. This should be threaded from the side of the needle which is grooved.

3)   The lower thread must be brought up through the needle hole in the throat plate.

To do this, hold the thread from the needle taut, turn the balance wheel towards the worker so that the take up lever goes down and up once. A gentle tug on the needle thread should reveal a loop of thread from spool in the needle hole of the throat plate. Place both threads under the presser foot and place towards back of machine.

Test the machine stitch

Place a double piece of material under the presser foot, lower the presser bar and machine about 10 cms of stitching. Examine the stitching.

The type of material used will determine the size and tension of the machine stitch. Smaller stitches (i.e. the greater number of stitches per cm) should be used on fine materials and larger stitches on thicker materials. Turning the stitch length knob to right or left will alter the stitch length. On some machines this control is in the form of a lever.

The wrong length of stitch will cause the fabric to pucker.

If the tension is correct, the stitch should appear the same on both sides. Generally it is easier to alter the upper thread tension by means of the tension knob. If the top tension is too tight the lower thread will loop through to the upper surface. If the upper tension is too loose, the top thread will loop through on the underside.

Top surface

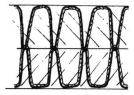 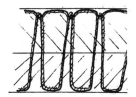 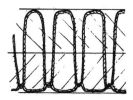

Underside

   Correct tension   *Top tension too tight*   *Top tension too loose*

Effects of different tension on the finished stitch

Working the machine

1)   Use the machine in a good light and on a table which is of a comfortable height.

2)   Keep the feet off the foot control when not actually sewing.

3)   If possible arrange most of the work to the left of the needle, lower the needle into desired position, lower presser foot and start to stitch.

4)   The edges of the presser foot can be used as a guide when machining; never watch the needle. There is no need to exert any pressure with the fingers when guiding as the presser foot and the feed dog will draw the material through at the correct rate.

5)   To turn a sharp corner, stop with the needle in the material, raise the presser foot, turn work to new direction, lower presser foot and carry on machining.

6)   To machine round a curve, pivot the work round the left or right hand according to the curve.

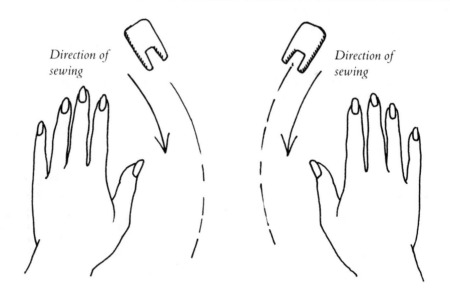

Direction of sewing

Direction of sewing

Pivot hand in anti clockwise direction

Pivoting fabric to curve stitching

Pivot hand in clockwise direction

7)   When line of machining is finished, move thread take up lever to its highest position, raise the presser foot, draw work to back of machine until there are about 20 cms of thread from material to machine. Cut in the middle.

8)   The threads at a raw edge may be tied and cut off, but where the threads end in the middle of the material they must be fastened off securely. The best method is to thread the ends into a needle and sew them through the machining. The stitches have been greatly enlarged for clarity in the diagram.

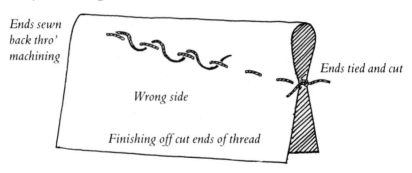

Ends sewn back thro' machining

Ends tied and cut

Wrong side

Finishing off cut ends of thread

Making the machine go where the worker wants it to go, does not come easily to everyone. Extra practice in guiding can be gained economically by machining on paper without any thread in the machine. Practice straight lines first, then sharp corners and then curves. Remember practice makes perfect and machining is a skill which once learnt is not forgotten.

When the machine won't work don't panic. Using the following table check for faults systematically and try again.

	Fault	Cause
1.	Stitch loopy on upper side	Incorrect threading or upper thread tension too tight.
2.	Stitch loopy on under side	Incorrect threading or top tension too loose or bobbin incorrectly placed.
3.	Stitches are missed	Needle bent or blunt. Material being pulled through dog feed. Thread too thick for needle.
4.	Thread breaking	Incorrect threading. Upper tension too tight. Needle bent or blunt. Spool too full. Thread caught on rough edge of cotton reel.
5.	Puckered Seams	Stitch too long. Upper tension too tight. Needle blunt.
6.	Broken needle	Presser foot loose. Material too thick for size of needle. Needle loose. Pins left in material. Knots left in tacking cotton.

7.	Material not moving through dog feed	Dog feed dropped. Stitch length regulator at its shortest. Too great a thickness of material.
8.	Needle not moving	Stop motion screw in balance wheel may be loose. Thread may be jammed in spool case.
9.	Light not working	Bulb broken. Fault in electric wiring.
10.	No power on machine	Fuse in plug broken. Break in wire. Power cut on mains.
11.	Machine works on its own	Condenser in foot control broken.
12.	Machine seems noisy and to be working heavily	Clean and oil machine.

Common Faults with Sewing Machines

General Care of machine

1) Clean and oil regularly as described in instruction booklet.

2) Have the machine serviced professionally from time to time. The frequency will depend on amount of use the machine gets.

3) Never work the machine when threaded without material under the lowered presser foot as this causes the two threads to jam in the spool case.

4) Always check that parts which are meant to be screwed on firmly are securely in place, e.g. a loose presser foot will quickly result in a broken needle.

5) Don't leave loose pins on the machine as these could cause serious damage to working parts if they become trapped inside the mechanism.

6) Keep covered when not in use, leaving the presser foot lowered onto material.

7) Check that flex and plugs on electric machine are in good order.

Machine Needles and Thread

Machine needles range from size 9 (fine) to 18 (thick) or 60 to 100 for continental sizes of needles. For synthetic jersey knit fabrics it is advisable to use a ball point needle which can be purchased.
These part the fabric threads without piercing them and help to prevent seam pucker.
Special needles are also available for sewing dress weight leather.

Needle Size	Weight of Material	Suggested Thread
9 - 11 (60 - 70)	Fine silks, nylons, lawn, georgette etc.	60 - 100 cotton, pure silk, drima.
14 (80)	General domestic cottons, light woollens, shirtings etc.	50 cotton 50 sylko Drima
16 - 18 (90 - 100)	Heavy cotton (Denim) Tweeds Suiting	40 cotton 40 sylko

Needles and thread for different fabrics

2

TERMS CONNECTED WITH FABRIC

Fabric Widths

Material may be purchased in a variety of widths. It is important to check the width of the material one chooses as this will affect the amount of material required for the chosen article or garment.

Metric	Imperial	Fabric Type
60cm 80cm	23″ 30″	Some interfacings
70cm	27″	Some hand woven material e.g. Harris Tweed and some embroidery fabrics.
90cm 115cm	35″/36″ 44″/45″	Mainly cottons and fine fabrics
140cm 150cm 165cm	54″/55″ 59″/60″ 65″	Mainly woollen type and jersey knit fabrics

Main widths available

Terms connected with weave and finish

Warp is the thread which runs the length of the material and is the strongest thread in the fabric.

Selvedges are the warp threads at the sides of the material and lie closer to one another than the rest of the warp threads.

Weft is the thread that is woven across the warp threads.

True Cross is formed when the warp threads are folded over and placed along the weft threads.

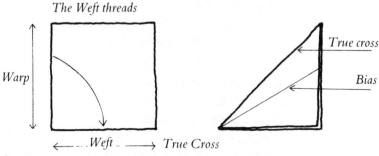

Bias lies between the true cross and the warp or the weft.

Plain Weave. In this type of fabric the weft (picks) pass regularly over one and then under one warp (ends) thread (Picks and ends are terms used in the weaving industry). On the next row the weft thread passes under and over the warp threads.

Twill Weave. In this weave the weft threads over and under the same number of warp threads (2, 3 or 4 or more) but on the second row the pattern slips one thread to the left. The right side of a twill weave may be recognised as the twill appears to climb upwards from left to right between the selvedge threads.

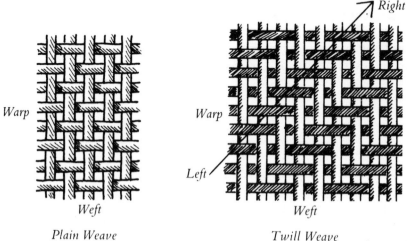

Plain Weave   Twill Weave

Satin Weave. In this weave the weft threads always pass over more warp threads than they pick up. The long threads on the right side give a smooth shiny effect to the fabric.

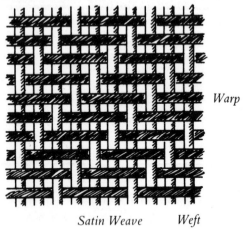

Warp

Satin Weave   Weft

Pile Fabrics. An extra thread is woven into the weft or warp of a plain fabric to make loops. These may be left uncut as in terry towelling or cut as in velvet type fabrics.

Nap. This refers to the pile on fabrics which lies all in one direction. Garments made up in napped fabrics must be cut so that the pile on all sections of the garment lie in the same direction.

Brushed Fabrics. These have had the surface raised by brushing on one side and when cutting out, this material should also be treated as having a 'nap' on it.

One-way Patterns. Some fabrics have printed patterns with a definite top and bottom and all facing the same way. This fabric should also be treated in the same way as napped fabrics when cutting out.

3

STITCHES USED IN DRESSMAKING

Stitches used in dressmaking may be classified into three groups:-

Temporary	Joining	Neatening
Tacking Basting Tailor Tacking	Running stitch Back stitch Machining Oversewing	Hemming Slip hemming Catch Stitch ZigZag 3 step zigzag Buttonholing

Three groups of Stitches

General rules for stitches

1) Use correct size needle and thread for fabric being used.
2) Fasten on and off securely. Never use a knot as these are liable to come undone.
3) Work one stitch at a time and aim to keep all stitches the same size.

Tacking – even

1) Use tacking cotton to contrast with material being sewn.
2) Begin and end with a firm double stitch (i.e. 2 small stitches on top of each other).
3) Work from right to left and take one stitch at a time.
4) When used for holding seams, the tacking should be worked where it is intended to machine. Even if the machining occasionally goes through the tacking stitches, the latter are still easy to remove as the

tacking cotton will break easily.

5) For tacking hems in position, tack near enough to the fold of the hem to hold both turnings.

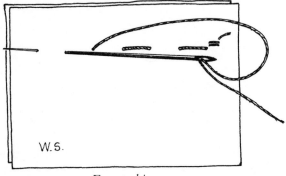

Even tacking

Tacking – Long and Short

This produces a firmer stitch suitable for heavier materials. It is quicker to work as two small stitches are taken on the needle at the same time.

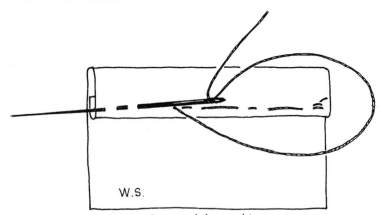

Long and short tacking

Diagonal Basting

1. This is used to hold two or more layers of material together to prevent them slipping while final stitching is being done, e.g. pleats, collars, waistbands etc.

2. It is always worked flat on the working surface, and usually from top to bottom but sometimes it is more convenient to work from bottom to top.

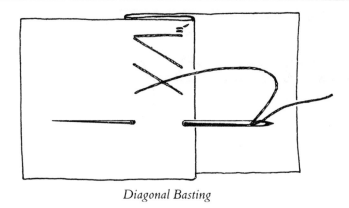

Diagonal Basting

Tailor Tacks

1. These are used to transfer important points and lines on the pattern to the material, e.g. seam lines, darts, buttonholes.
2. Always use double tacking cotton of contrasting colour. As the cotton gets used up fairly quickly, use a rather longer thread in the needle (about 40cm when doubled), but beware of having too long a thread as this merely tangles up.
3. Knots and double stitches are NOT required to begin and end this stitch.

To mark a long line

1. This is a much looser stitch than an even tacking stitch.
2. The needle passes through paper pattern and both layers of fabric and the stitches are about the same size as even tacking stitches.
3. It is important that loops of thread about 2.5cm long are left between each stitch.
4. When all the tailor tacks have been put in, the loops are cut so that the paper pattern may be removed.
5. The two layers of material are then very carefully separated and the threads between are cut.
   The straight line is now marked on both pieces of the section of pattern in exactly the same way.

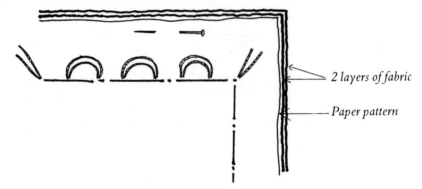

2 layers of fabric

Paper pattern

Marking a long line with Tailor tacks

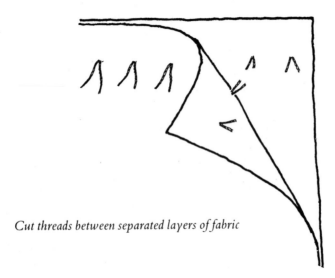

Cut threads between separated layers of fabric

To mark a single dot or perforation

1. Use double cotton as before.
2. Take a small double stitch through the pattern and two layers of the fabric. Too big a stitch will not mark the place accurately. Leave an end of 2.5cms.
3. Take a second stitch in exactly the same place, leaving a loop of about 2.5cms. as the thread is pulled through.
4. Leave an end of 2.5cms. and cut off thread. Cut loop.
5. Proceed to next dot and repeat process until all dots are marked.
6. Remove pattern and carefully separate layers of fabric to cut threads between them.

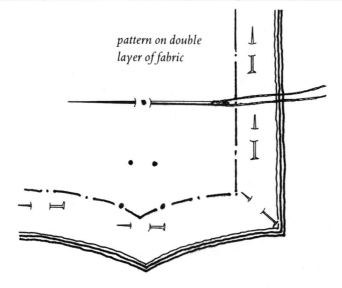

*pattern on double
layer of fabric*

Marking a single dot or perforation

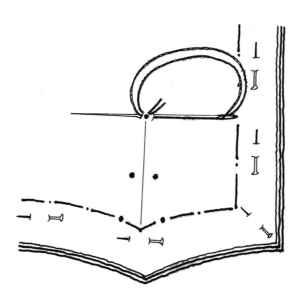

Take a small double stitch

Repeat until all dots are marked

All joining and neatening stitches should be worked in a thread which matches the material in colour, fibre content and thickness.

Running stitch

1. Begin and end with a double stitch.
2. Work from right to left.
3. Take one stitch at a time, the space between each stitch being equal in length to the stitch. This should be no more than 2mm.

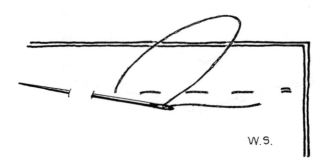

W.S.

Running Stitch

Back Stitch

On the side on which it is worked, this stitch should resemble a machine stitch. It is a much stronger stitch than running stitch when the stitches are of a comparable size. It is used for joining two pieces of material together.

1. Begin and end with a double stitch.
2. Work from right to left.
3. Take one running stitch.
4. The needle goes back to the last stitch and forward the same distance beyond the thread.

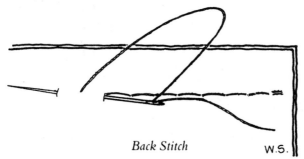

Back Stitch   W.S.

Machining

This replaces backstitching in much of modern dressmaking as, not only is it quicker to do, it is also much stronger. However, it is essential that the correct stitch and tension are used for the material, otherwise the stitch may not be strong.

The ends of cotton must be firmly sewn off when the machining finishes in the middle of the material. Where it finishes at the edge of the material the ends of the thread may be tied together and cut off.

Oversewing

This is used to join two folded edges of material together as at the end of a hem. The stitches should be very small.

1. To begin, slip the thread between the folds of the fabric and then work over it.
2. Work from right to left.
3. Put the needle in from back to front and at right angles to the folded edge.

4.   To end, work back over the last 3 or 4 stitches.

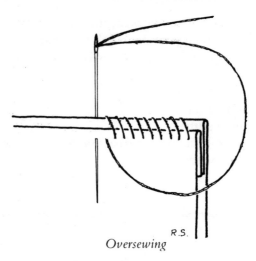

Oversewing

Hemming

This is a very small stitch and is most often used on flat articles and some children's clothes.
1.   Begin thread by running in fold of hem.
2.   Work from right to left. The hem is held over the fingers and the rest of the garment towards the worker.
3.   A very small slanting stitch is taken just beneath the hem and just into the fold of the hem.
4.   The stitches are very tiny indeed and should hardly show on either side of the hem.

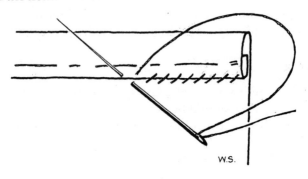

Hemming

Slip Hemming

This is much quicker to work than hemming and is more often used as it is also easier to get a professional finish to hems.

It is essential to take only one stitch at a time and care must be taken not to pull the stitch too tight as this will cause a ridge on the right side of the garment. Too loose a stitch will not secure the hem properly.

When the hem is folded back to its proper position none of the stitching should be visible.

1. Fasten the thread with a double stitch in the fold of the Lem.
2. Work from right to left.
3. The hem is folded back away from the worker.
4. The needle picks up just one thread of the garment.
5. The needle is then passed along the fold of the hem for about 1.0cm.

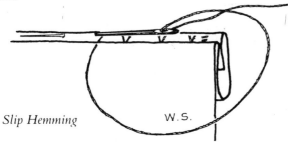

Slip Hemming   W.S.

Catch Stitch

Used on hems on thicker materials which are too thick to take a double turning on the hem.

1. The stitch may be worked over the hem, or between hem and garment.
2. Work from right to left.
3. Begin and end with a double stitch in hem.
4. Take a small stitch in the garment and then in hem.

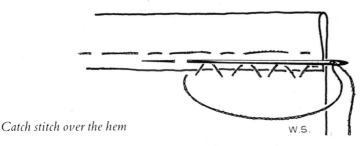

Catch stitch over the hem   W.S.

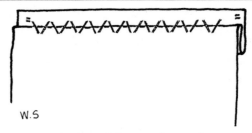

W.S

Catch stitch between hem and garment

Zigzag Stitch

This is used to neaten an edge on woven fabric.

1. The stitch width control is set to between 2 and 4 depending on the thickness of the material.
    The stitch length should be left at the normal length for the material being sewn.
2. The edge to be zigzagged is trimmed to an even width.
    Ensure that there is a clean edge.
3. The material should be put under the presser foot so that the stitch goes over the edge of the material.

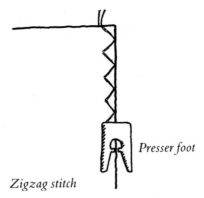

Presser foot

Zigzag stitch

3-step Zigzag or Multi Stitch Zigzag

This stitch sews 3 stitches in one direction and then 3 stitches the other way.

It has much more 'give' in it than ordinary zigzag and is therefore often used on jersey knit fabrics.

Because it does several stitches in each direction, it is very useful on loosely woven tweed type materials in order that the coarse threads may be fastened in.

The stitch selector is turned to 3 step zigzag and the stitch width and length control set as for zigzag.

The stitch should be worked close to the trimmed edge.

Three step zigzag stitch

Buttonholing

This stitch is used over raw edges, usually double. The obvious place is on buttonholes, but it may be used elsewhere.

Practice in a thick thread first and practice getting the stitches even in size and spacing.

1. The edge is held away from the worker.
2. It is worked from left to right.
3. The needle must be placed behind the edge and brought out at front of material.
4. Keep single thread on left hand side and place the double thread from the eye of the needle so that it passes under the needle from left to right.
5. The needle is then pulled through the material and away from the worker so that the knot formed sits on the raw edge.

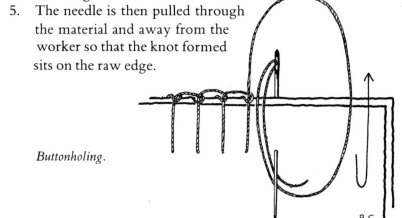

Buttonholing.

R.S.

Arrow shows direction in which needle is pulled

4

PERSONAL MEASUREMENTS

When making garments for a particular person the individual measures of the person must be checked against those of the pattern being used. Very few people are exactly stock-size and it is much easier to alter the paper pattern than to have to take remedial action once the actual construction of the garment has begun.

For most garments, measures should be taken over a thin slip with the model in well fitting foundation garments if these are usually worn. The model should stand naturally but without stooping or standing unevenly.

A thin piece of string or wool tied round the waist will define the natural waistline clearly.

As many measures as possible are taken from the back, but some are necessarily taken from the front. When taking measures which go round the body, keep two fingers inside the tape measure to avoid pulling too tight.

It is usual when taking the inside leg measurement to ask the model to place the end of the tape at the crutch so that the other end of the tape may be guided accurately to the ankle bone.

In many cases all these measurements will not be needed but they are included here for the sake of completeness.

Measurement	Taken from

1. Nape of neck to waist
2. a.b.c. Waist to hem
3. Bust – fullest part,
   slightly higher at back
4. Waist
5. Hips – fullest part of seat.
   18–24cm below waist.
6. Width across back.
	Measures taken from back

7 . Width across chest 8. Inside arm length 9. Round upper arm 10. Round wrist 11. Inside leg length 12. Thigh measures	Measures taken from front
13. Crotch depth for trousers	Taken seated on table

Taking measures

Numbered measurement locations

correspond with table above

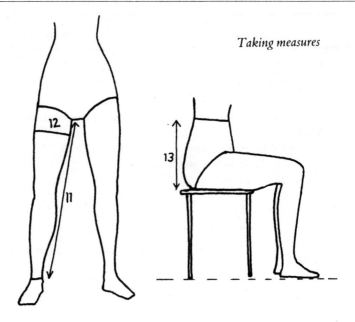

Taking measures

5

CHOICE OF COMMERCIAL PATTERNS

Type of Pattern

There are many makes of pattern from which the home dressmaker can choose, some with important points marked by perforations in the paper and others with these points printed onto the pattern itself sometimes in several languages. It is very much easier for the novice to follow a pattern with the details printed on the pattern but the novice should be wary of what the manufacturers term multi-size patterns where several sizes are superimposed on the one pattern piece. This can be very confusing as the printing of the seam-allowance line is usually sacrificed.

The more expensive patterns may very well use more paper, as in an evening dress, or require more complicated pattern construction. They also tend to have more detailed instruction sheets to direct the maker through the various stages of construction, again of particular help to the novice.

Many manufacturers design patterns especially for beginners and these are usually advertised as 'Easy to Sew'.

Size of Pattern

It helps considerably to work from a pattern which is the correct size or very nearly the correct size.

The bust measurement is usually used to get the size for garments worn above or partly above the waist.

The hip measurement and sometimes the waist measurement is used for garments worn below the waist.

Manufacturers cut patterns with sufficient fullness to allow for ease of movement for each particular size so that there is no need to allow for this when taking measures. But it must be taken into consideration when checking personal measures against those of the pattern.

The following amounts are usually allowed for ease:

7cms on bust measurement

5cms on waist measurement

7cms on hip measurement

The height of the person will also affect the proportions of the various parts of the pattern. The main figure types can be seen on the following table.

Main Figure Types

Type	Height in metres	Characteristics of Type
Misses	1.65 – 1.68	Well proportioned figure
Womens	1.65 – 1.68	Larger more mature figure
Miss Petite	1.57 – 1.63	For the shorter but developed figure
Half Size	1.57 – 1.60	For the developed figure which is short from nape to waist
Young Junior Teen	1.55 – 1.60	For the developing figure with high bust line
Chubbie	1.32 – 1.55	For the growing figure which is over average weight for height
Girls	1.27 – 1.55	Immature figure with no bust line
Childrens Toddlers Babies	.79 – 1.17 .71 – 1.02 .31 – .61	Sizes usually refer to age of child – but this can be misleading if child is large for age
Boys and Teen Boys	1.22 – 1.73	Compare to Girls sizes
Men	1.78	Average mature adult

The pattern envelope should be studied carefully to find the following information:

1) The actual size of the pattern
2) Front and back view of the garments
3) Description of fashion features on garments
4) Amount of material required
5) Table of measures for all sizes in which pattern is made
6) Suggested fabrics for garment
7) Extra items needed to make garment.

How to work out how much fabric required ★View 1. Size 12. 165cm fabric. Amount shown in box.

Fabric Reqd	Size 10	12	14	16
View 1 90cm				
140cm				
165cm		★		
View 2. 90cm				
140cm				
165cm				

Fabric requirements table on pattern envelope

Understanding the Pattern

With the help of the instruction sheet, sometimes called the Primer, identify the various sections of the pattern.

It may well be that there are several styles in the chosen pattern, so select the pieces needed for the style that is going to be made. This information is usually noted on the instruction sheet.

View 1 . . . Use pattern pieces A.B.C.D. and E
View 2 . . . Use pattern pieces A.B.C. and D

Put pattern pieces not required back into the envelope.

Pattern Markings

These do vary slightly according to the make of pattern but the important ones are very similar and are shown on the following table.

Meaning	Printed Pattern	Perforated Pattern
Straight grain of fabric	Long black arrow	3 evenly spaced large holes
Place to fold of fabric	Arrow with curved ends	
Matching balance points on edge	Black diamonds on edge of pattern	Notches along edge of pattern
Seam allowance – usually 1.5cm from edge	Solid line is cutting line Broken line is seam line	Series of small evenly spaced holes
Dart	Black dots arranged in a triangle	Holes arranged in a triangle

Preparing the Pattern for Cutting Out

1) Check the pattern measures against personal measures plus allowances for ease. Remember that it is usual for only half the pattern to
   be supplied as double material is usually used for cutting out.
   Therefore either the pattern measures must be doubled or the
   personal measures plus allowances for ease must be halved.

2) Make any alterations that are necessary to the pattern. These may
   be due to differences in shape from the stock size figure for which
   commercial patterns are planned, e.g. hips may be larger in
   proportion than bust.

Small Alterations up to 2cms may be made at the side edges of the
pattern e.g. a skirt waist which is 2cms too small can be increased by
adding 0.5cm to side of front pattern and 0.5cm to side of back pattern
above and below the waist.

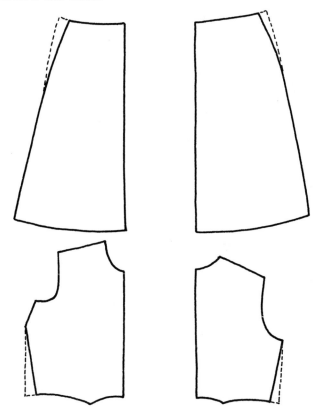

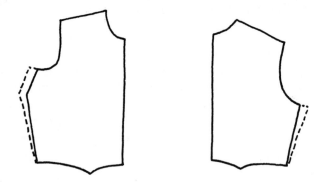

Increasing patterns by small amounts at waist of skirt and bodice and at bust.

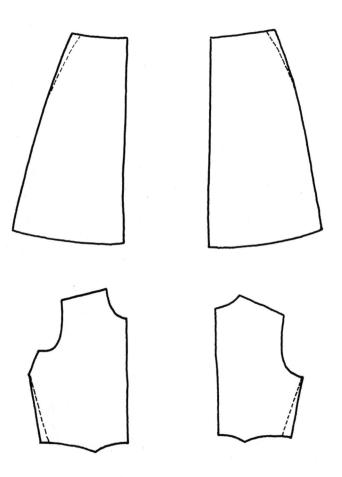

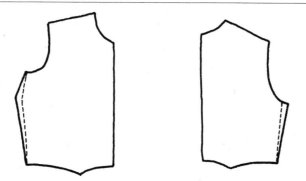

Reducing patterns by small amounts at skirt and bodice waist and at bust

Larger alterations must be made through the body of the pattern but without drastically altering the shape and style lines of pattern.

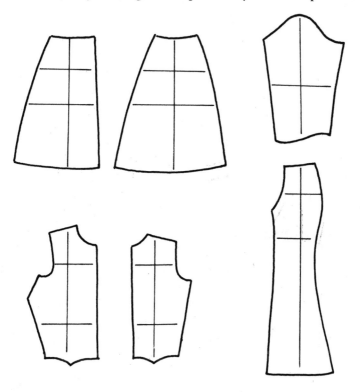

Position of alterations on pattern pieces

Width is altered at vertical lines on diagrams. These are always parallel to straight grain lines.

Length is altered at horizontal lines. These are very often marked on paper patterns.

A reduction in width or length is achieved by taking a tuck in the pattern, remembering that a tuck 1.5cm deep reduces the pattern by 3.0cms. In putting a tuck in a shaped pattern piece the seam line becomes stepped and needs to be corrected.

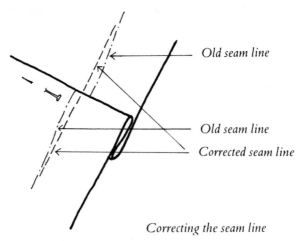

Old seam line

Old seam line

Corrected seam line

Correcting the seam line

An increase in width or length is achieved by cutting the pattern along the appropriate line. Pin an extra piece of paper between the two pieces of pattern, making the space between the two pieces equal to the amount by which the pattern piece is to be increased. Re-shape fitting line.

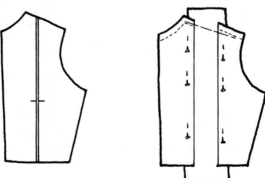

Pattern cut and balance mark put in. Paper let in and shoulder seamline re-shaped.

3) It is often easier for the beginner to trim a printed pattern on the thick black cutting line, but this is not essential unless the material is thick or slippery.

4) Iron pattern with warm iron.

Preparing the Material

1) **Straighten the cut edges of the fabric.** This may be done by tearing off a narrow strip or pulling a weft thread out and cutting along the gap it has left.

2) **Fold the material.** For speed and accuracy it is usual to cut on double material wherever possible and to make sure a pair of any section is cut. There are three main types of fold.

   The appropriate way of folding is selected from the layout charts according to style, size and fabric width and whether fabric being used has a nap.

Selvedges together →

Fold →

Lengthways or warp fold

Selvedge →

These distances must be the same length

Fold →

Partial lengthways fold

2 Selvedges →

Crossways or weft fold

2 Selvedges →

3. Pull the fabric straight if necessary. Even though the ends of the fabric have been carefully cut or torn to the weft thread, when the material is folded it appears not to lie straight.

This is because the material has been stretched unevenly as it has been baled. If this has happened it is a fairly simple job to pull the material in the opposite direction to get it to lie straight.

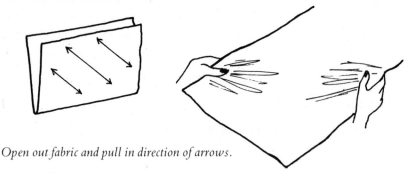

Open out fabric and pull in direction of arrows.

Lay on the pattern

1) Using the layout chart already selected for folding the material, try a rough layout to see how the pattern pieces are going to fit on the fabric. Lay the largest pieces first and fit the small pieces round them.

2) Make sure that the straight grain of each piece runs parallel to the selvedges of fabric. To be sure that this is accurate a measurement should be taken from each end of the straight grain arrow to the selvedge.

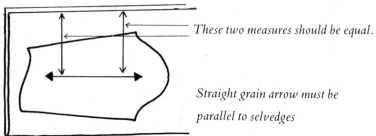

These two measures should be equal.

Straight grain arrow must be parallel to selvedges

3) Any edge of pattern which represents a fold should be placed exactly to a fold.

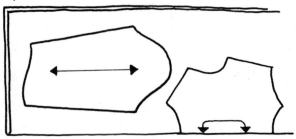

Place fold arrow exactly to fabric fold

Pin on the pattern

1) When the pattern is satisfactorily positioned, pin each end of straight grain arrow to prevent pattern slipping off grain. Now check accuracy of this line again.
   If the pattern has an edge that is placed to a fold, pin this first as it is also on the straight grain.
2) Now smooth out from the straight grain line or fold line and pin to material keeping both quite flat. On NO account must the material be lifted to insert a pin.
3) Too many pins will ruck the material and too few will not hold the pattern securely.
4) Do not pin too near the edge of pattern but inside the margin for seam allowance.

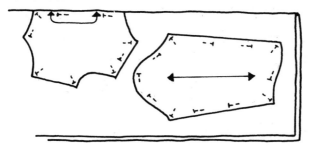

Pin inside seam allowance margin. Note placing of pins at corners of pattern pieces.

Special Considerations for Check Fabrics

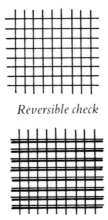

Reversible check

Non-reversible check

Look carefully at the check to decide if it is a reversible check as in the diagram.

In this case the pattern pieces may be placed without regard to a one way pattern.

Other checks, often traditional tartans are not reversible and must be treated in the same way as napped fabric when laying on pattern pieces.

The checks must be arranged so that they match at shoulder, side seams, centre front, centre back and sleeve.

This is done by making sure the balance points, on say both sides of a shoulder seam, lie on exactly the same part of the check. It is of course extremely important that the material is folded exactly with checks matching otherwise the careful placing of the pattern on the top side of the fabric is lost on the underside.

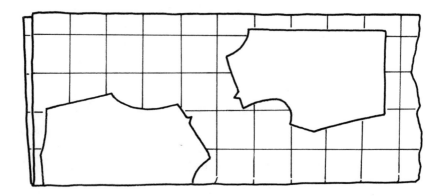

Both sides of shoulder seam lie on the same part of the check

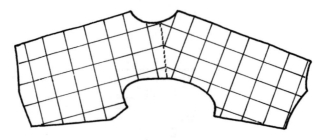

So when the seam is sewn the checks will match

The same principle of matching balance points applies wherever there is a seam in checks. It does require a great deal of patience and thought at this stage, but once the garment is cut out, bad planning cannot be rectified. It will be appreciated that the bigger the check the more material will be needed to make the checks match.

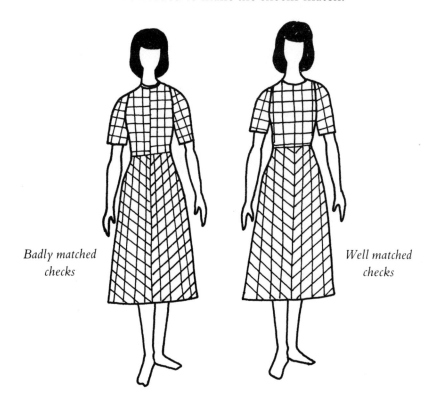

*Badly matched
checks*

*Well matched
checks*

Cutting Out

1) Re-check layout.
2) Cut along the cutting line indicated on the pattern or at an even distance from the edge if a pattern is being used on which there are no seam allowances. These could be marked in with tailors' chalk if wished.
3) Put left hand on pattern to steady it.
4) Using large scissors, held correctly, cut with long even strokes.
5) Balance points and notches should be cut outwards, using points of scissors to save threadmarking them later.

6)   Never lift or move material when cutting out.

7)   When all pieces are cut out make a neat bundle of the left over bits, discarding any that are very small.

Transferring marks to material

1. Tailor Tacking

Dart tailor tacked.

This method transfers the seam lines and style lines to both pieces of fabric at the same time, thus ensuring that both pieces of a section of garment are identical.

For speed it isn't always necessary to mark the whole length of a line, just the top and the bottom.

If there are a lot of markings on a particular section it could be helpful to a beginner if a different colour thread is used for each set of marks, e.g. red for darts, green for seam allowances and so on.

It is helpful for fitting to put a line of even tacking stitches down centre front and centre back.

When all the pattern pieces have been tailor tacked remove pins and lift off pattern.

Carefully cut between layers.

half back bodice with tailor tacks

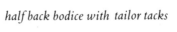

2. With dressmakers' carbon paper

This method is not successful for all fabrics, e.g. pile fabrics and thick woollens. Experiment first on scraps of fabric before embarking on this method.

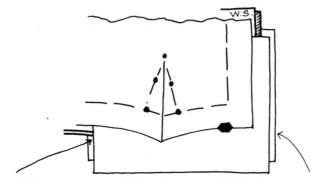

Carbon laid on wrong side of fabric when material folded wrong side out with 2 pieces of fabric between the carbons.

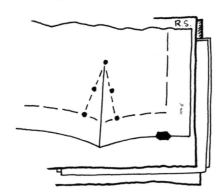

Carbon placed to wrong side of fabric when fabric folded right side out with 2 pieces of carbon between the fabric.

a. The carbon markings must be on wrong side of fabric.
b. Lay section to be marked flat on a firm surface such as the table protected by cardboard.
c. Take out pins from one part of section and lay 2 pieces of carbon paper shiny side down on 2 wrong sides of material.
d. Fold back pattern to original position and trace over style lines with blunt instrument e.g. wooden meat skewer, empty biro.
e. When this portion is completely marked remove carbons, re-pin

pattern to portion just marked and proceed to next portion of section.

f. It is important to see that at no time during the marking by this method are all the pins removed at once. It is difficult and time consuming to try and get the pattern back in exactly the same position. Only remove all pins when marking is complete.

6

CONSTRUCTION OF GARMENT

If the pattern has been carefully checked against personal measurements and altered where necessary, there should be no need to do any further fitting. However, if there are figure faults which make the body asymmetrical, it is a good idea to tack the garment together and try it on.

There are two main methods of constructing clothes, the 'flat' method and the 'round' method. Both are equally acceptable providing accuracy is maintained but there are distinct advantages in the 'flat' method for the beginner as the work can be spread out more easily to see where each piece goes.

Flat method – General order of Work for dress

1. Back darts, seams and fastening ⎤
⎥ There will not necessarily be
2. Front darts, seams and fastening ⎦ all of these
3. Shoulder seam
4. Neck finish
5. Armhole facing or sleeve
6. Underarm and side seams
7. Hems on sleeves and lower edge

Round method – General order of Work for dress

1. Fix together each main section
   e.g. Bodice – darts, yokes, pockets, seams (shoulder and side)
   Sleeves – seam, cuff or hem
   Skirt – darts, pockets, pleats, seams.

2. Fit together the smaller parts to the larger
    e.g. Collar to bodice
       Sleeves to bodice
       Bodice to skirt (if there is a waist seam)

Commercial patterns provide a very useful step by step guide through the construction of a particular garment. It is not the only method but is one which has been tried out, which works and is relatively simple to explain. There is very little room on an instruction sheet to deal with the finer points of garment construction and as experience is gained, the worker will be able to select the most appropriate method for the style and fabric in use, bringing a more critical approach to the craft.

7

ARRANGEMENT OF FULLNESS

Darts are found at:-

> Shoulder
>
> Bust
>
> Waist
>
> Elbows of fitted sleeves

They are used to give shape to a garment by taking in material at narrower parts of the body and tapering to the widest part.

A well stitched dart tapers off to nothing at the point so that there is no sudden burst of fullness at the end of the dart.

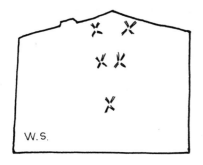 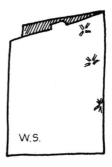

Darts are usually made on the wrong side of the material. The amount of material to be taken up by a dart is marked by a triangle of dots, the size of the triangle depending on the size of the dart. The triangle of dots is accurately folded in half along its length. The two marks should lie on top of one another when folded.

Pin and tack along the pattern line of dart. Stitch the dart starting at the wide end and tapering to nothing at the point.

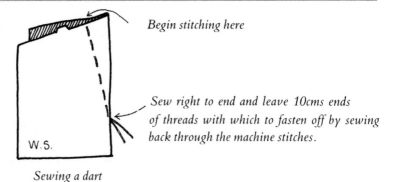

Begin stitching here

Sew right to end and leave 10cms ends of threads with which to fasten off by sewing back through the machine stitches.

Sewing a dart

A good shaped dart will follow the pattern line and not have a concave and convex curve in it. Press the dart to one side. If using thick material slit dart along fold and press apart.

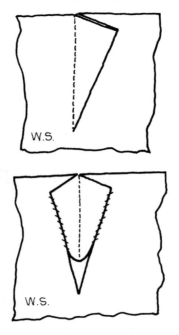

Press dart to one side or slit and press apart

A dart pointed at both ends may present some difficulties to a beginner as it is difficult to start machining at the narrow end of a dart and get a good shape. If this is so, start machining at widest part, machine to one end, go back to middle and machine to other end.

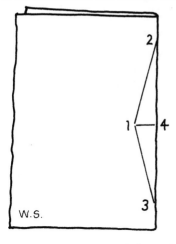

Machine 1 – 2 (leave 10cms ends of threads)
Machine 1 – 3 (leave 10cms ends of threads)

If the dart is very wide at 1, it may be necessary to snip at 4 so that the dart may be pressed flat (Neaten cut edges at 4 with buttonhole stitch)

A dart pointed at both ends

Tucks are small stitched folds of fabric and serve several purposes.
1. If placed on the front shoulder or waist of a blouse they will give extra fullness to the bust.
2. If stitched the whole length of a garment, they are regarded as a fashion feature.
3. They may be used to allow for growth.

The actual size of the tuck varies enormously, from 1mm up to several cms. They are shown on printed patterns by two parallel lines and usually have an arrow linking them.

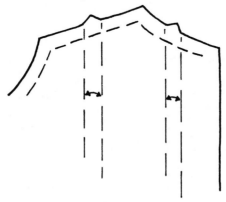

Arrowed parallel lines on pattern to locate tucks.

Tucks are usually made on the right side of the material and may be stitched by hand, using a very small running stitch or by machine.

If there are several tucks to be made on a garment, it is easier for the beginner to fix and stitch one tuck at a time as the work curls and becomes difficult to handle if all are fixed before stitching.

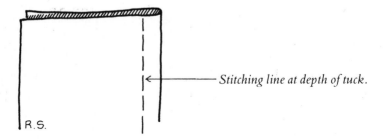

Stitching line at depth of tuck.

R.S.

Tucks are usually made on the right side of the material

Tucks must be stitched at an even width all the way down the tuck if they are to look professional. Where there are groups of tucks to be made a machine tucking attachment is useful.

Machine tucking attachment

Where tucks are a fashion feature, they may be arranged in any number of ways.

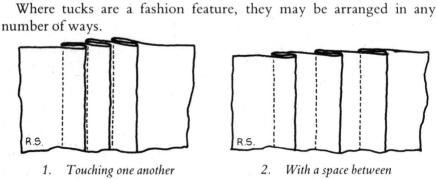

R.S.

R.S.

1.   *Touching one another*   2.   *With a space between*

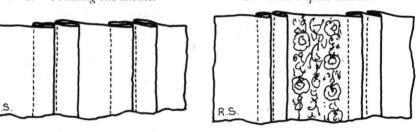

R.S.

R.S.

3.   *In groups*   4.   *Used in conjunction with lace or tatting*

Where there is a large area to be pin-tucked it is sometimes an advantage to put the pin tucks in the material before cutting out. This is especially true if the tucks are added at the discretion of the worker. Decide how close the tucks are to be and draw threads out to represent the fold of the tucks. This will not be noticeable when the tucks are stitched and pressed. When pin tucking on fabric is complete, press all tucks to one side fold fabric on straight grain and pin pattern on in usual way.

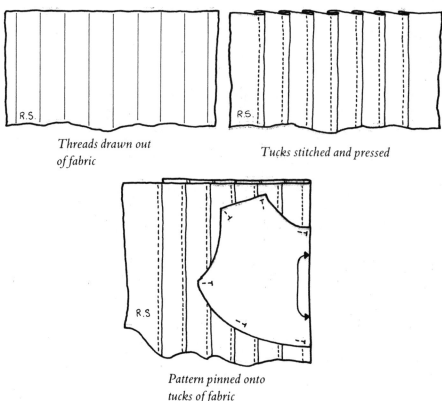

Threads drawn out of fabric

Tucks stitched and pressed

Pattern pinned onto tucks of fabric

Gathers and Easing. This method of controlling fullness is most effective when used on soft fine materials which will gather well. When estimating the fullness of a pattern piece measure the piece that is to be gathered (A) and the piece that it is to be set into it. (B) In very full gathers A is equal to 3 times B. A medium amount of fullness is achieved by having A = 1½ × B. Anything less than A = 1½ × B is generally termed as easing.

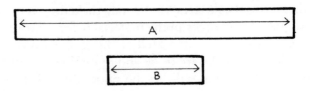

'A' can be gathered or eased into 'B'

Gathers. May be worked by hand or machine

Hand Gathers

1. Use sewing thread of matching colour
2. Begin with a very firm double stitch
3. Work first row running stitch on seam line and between the marks for the gathers. Do not fasten off but leave 10cms of thread hanging.
4. Work second row of running stitch 3mm above the first row (i.e. in the seam allowance).

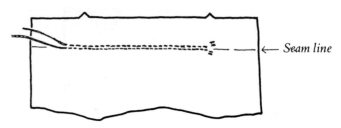

Work 2 rows of running stitch

5. Pull the gathers up to the required length and secure ends around a pin in figure of 8 movement. Spread gathers evenly.

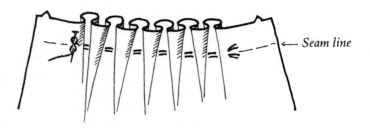

Draw up and spread gathers

Machine Gathers

1. The machine stitch regulator is set to produce its longest stitch and the tension regulator to a fairly loose tension so that the top thread just begins to loop to the underneath.
2. Machine 2 rows in the same position as for hand gathering.
3. Now pull the two lower threads till the required length is reached and proceed as for hand gathers.

   For very long lengths of gathering, the work is best divided up and then gathered in separate lengths to avoid breaking the thread when pulling up.

Easing is the term used to arrange slight amounts of fullness as in curved seams, elbows of fitted sleeves, sleeve heads. Expert workers can usually manage to cope with this slight amount of fullness by careful pinning but beginners will find it easier to put a single row of running stitches on the seam line. This can be pulled up to fit the other part of the seam, but care must be taken to see that there are no gathers in the resultant seam.

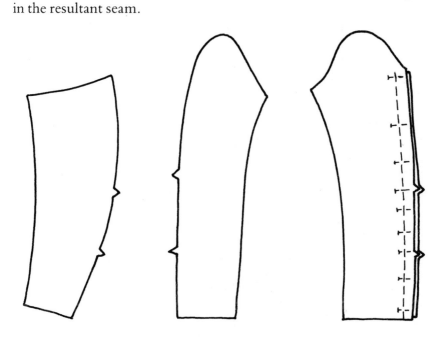

Fullness in one side of seam is eased to fit the other side

Smocking is a popular version of gathers which is often used on children's clothes. As it is essential to have the gathers evenly spaced in both directions, it is usual to buy transfers of smocking dots. The transfers are ironed onto the wrong side of the fabric. The gathers differ from normal gathers in that only the material marked by the dot is picked up on to the needle.

On very delicate fabrics the transfer is laid <u>under</u> the fabric and pinned securely in position but not ironed on, with wrong side facing upwards. The material over the dot is picked up onto the needle.

The gathers are pulled up to required width and secured in pairs at the one side. As pins are not suitable because of the further work on the gathers, the pairs of threads are knotted securely together. The top pair is then tied to the next pair and so on, for the whole depth of the smocking.

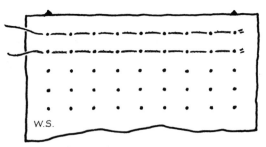

Partially prepared for smocking

Check fabric may also be used successfully for smocking and does away with the use of smocking dots. Consideration should be given to the construction of the check, e.g. on a 0.5cm blue and white check, if all the white checks are picked up onto the needle, the blue part of the check will become the background for the smocking, and vice versa.

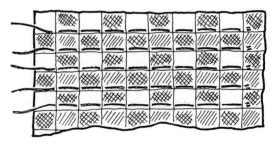

Gathering check fabric for smocking

Pleating Machines are also available. These pull up the fabric very quickly, but as the machines are rather expensive, a great deal of smocking would have to be undertaken to justify the purchase of such a machine.

The actual embroidery is worked on the right side and is usually based on variations of stem stitch. The important points to remember are that the needle is usually held at right angles to the folds formed by gathers and only the surface of the fold is picked up onto the needle.

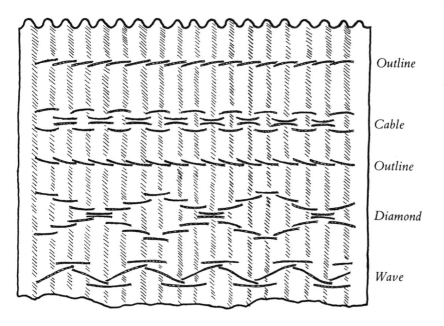

Outline

Cable

Outline

Diamond

Wave

Finished sample of smocking showing a variety of stitches, very much enlarged.

Pleats are folds of material designed to give extra fullness in a garment.

Pleats hang best in a firm, medium weight material without a crease resistant finish, otherwise they are difficult to press in without using an iron temperature that may damage the fabric.

They may be allowed to fall freely from a supporting seam or band, or they may be stitched down along a portion of their length.

There are 3 layers to a pleat, under, middle and top.

The main types of pleat are:-

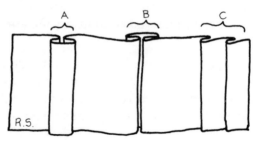

A – Box, B *– Inverted and* C *– Knife pleats*

It is possible to get material permanently pleated and this is the best method for sunray and accordian pleating where the folds of the pleat stand out from the material.

In accordian pleating the pleats are very fine.

In sunray pleating the size of the pleats varies but they always taper to nothing at the top.

To mark pleats. On paper patterns pleats are marked for their entire length. Two lines are used – one to mark the fold of the pleat and another to mark the line to which the fold should be placed. Both these lines should be marked onto the material by a suitable method, e.g. tailor tacking.

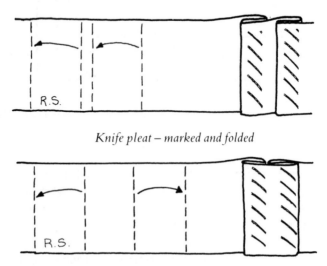

Knife pleat – marked and folded

Box pleat – marked and folded

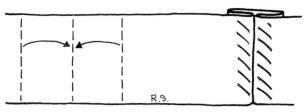

Inverted pleat – marked and folded

Inverted pleats are the ones most usually top stitched and this may be done in a variety of patterns.

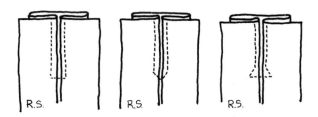

Top stitched inverted pleats

Inverted pleats may also be formed by stitching on the inside.

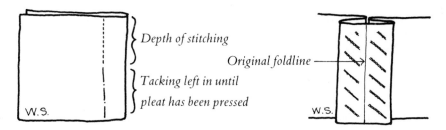

Inverted pleat stitched on the inside   *Inverted pleat opened out ready to press*

Open material and lay right side's down on a table and press the folded edge directly on to the line of stitching.
Pin and baste in position.

When pleats are made in very thick material the extra bulk caused can be eliminated by trimming away the excess material on the W.S. and replacing it with a piece of thin lining material in a toning colour.

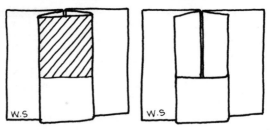

Cut away shaded portion from uppermost section of pleat only

Cut rectangle of lining material the size of the portion cut away and turnings of 1cm. Attach to lower cut edge.

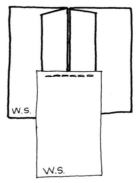

Cut and attach lining

Lift lining piece up and attach to sides of pleat by hand sewing or zigzag machining. As lining material tends to fray, it is advisable to turn in the edge once on the sides of the lining.

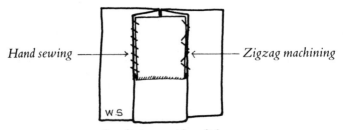

Sew lining to sides of pleat

Where a seam falls in a pleat, e.g. inverted pleat at the centre back of a skirt, the seam and pleat must be fixed into position for as far as possible, the hem finished according to the fabric and the seam and pleat then finished through both portions of hem.

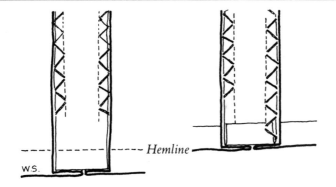

Finishing a pleat when it falls at a seam line

8

SEAMS

A seam is a joining of two pieces of material. Closely fitting clothes have more seams than loose ones as seams can be shaped and curved to help the garment fit snugly. Seams can be used to emphasise a particular style line or they may be almost invisible.

The type of seam chosen will depend on:-

        1 .The type of garment being made

        2. The type of material being used

        3. The technical skill of the worker

Characteristics of a well made seam

1. Should be strong in relation to fabric and garment.

2. Well stitched so that a good line is given to the garment.

3. Well pressed.

4. Flat and neat in appearance on both right and wrong sides.

5. Seams of the same kind on one garment should also be the same finished width.

6. When two seams meet or cross there should be a perfect match at the junction, as at side seam of waisted dress, crotch of trousers and often at underarm and sleeve seam.

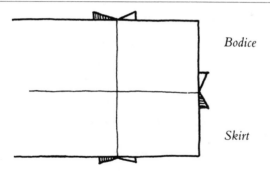

A perfect match at the junction

7. To avoid bulk at seams, trim away surplus wherever possible especially when two seams meet or cross.

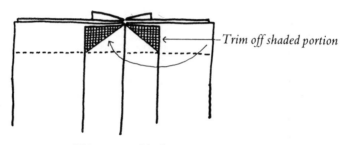

Trim to avoid bulk

Seam allowance is the amount of material outside the seam line that is allowed for making the seams. Most pattern manufacturers leave 1.5cm for this purpose, but if one is dealing with material which frays badly, it is quite permissible to increase this to 2.0cm.

Seam width sometimes called seam fell, is the finished width of the seam.

The Open or Plain Seam sometimes called the Dressmaker's Seam, is probably the simplest seam of all and can be used on many kinds of fabric and many garments. Usually no stitching shows on the right side, but some commercial patterns may indicate some top stitching as a style feature.

Directions for Making Open Seams.

1. Place right sides facing and match balance points carefully. If pattern lines are marked these should now lie on top of one another.

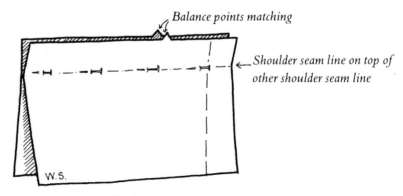

Balance points matching

←Shoulder seam line on top of other shoulder seam line

Ready to sew an open seam

2. Pin, tack and machine along seam line in a straight line or a good curve. When machining, start and finish as near to edges as possible, e.g neck and armhole edges.
3. Remove tacking.
4. If the seam is exposed it needs to be neatened by one of the following methods.

(a) **Edge stitching** – a very popular method for cotton and similar fabrics. With the tip of the iron, press a turning 3mm wide onto wrong side of each seam turning. Both sides of the seam should be exactly the same width for the whole length of the seam and the same width as other similar seams on the same garment.

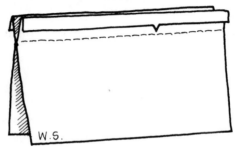

Press 3mm turning

The top edge of each side of the seam is machined and the extra material, including the balance point, is trimmed off.

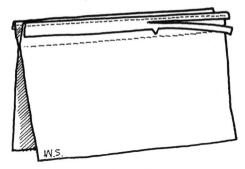

machine and trim edges

Press the seam open with machined turnings pressed inside. This leaves a neat finish and no edges to fray.

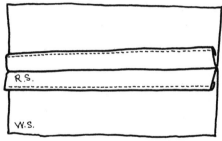

Press seam open

(b)   The seam turnings may be trimmed to an even width and then overcast, machined and overcast, zigzagged or bound with seam binding.

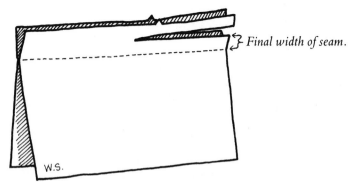

It is quicker and more accurate to trim both sides of the seam at the same time

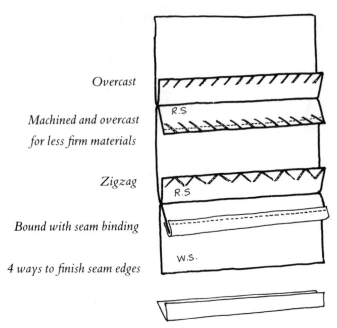

Overcast

Machined and overcast
for less firm materials

Zigzag

Bound with seam binding

4 ways to finish seam edges

Seam binding pressed ready for putting onto seam turning ready to be machined

Finally, when one or other of these 4 seam finishes has been completed, press the seam open.

Further Points about Open Seams

1. A seam which appears to hang crookedly could be caused by badly matched seams or poor machining.
2. Stripes or checks which do not match on right side have had insufficient care in preparation of the seam. A 'roller' foot is a good investment for machining stripes and checks as it helps prevent the top layer of material being pushed along over the bottom layer during machining, causing stripes and checks not to match.
3. Open seams which are very curved will not press flat unless the turnings are snipped.

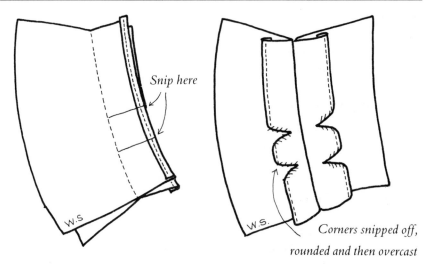

Snip here

*Corners snipped off,
rounded and then overcast*

Snip and neaten to allow curved seams to lie flat

4. On some materials the impressions of the seam turnings can be seen on the right side after pressing. This can be avoided by pressing the seam over a padded, rounded article such as a rolling pin, or by slipping thin card between the seam turning and garment before pressing.

A Welt Seam is very similar to an Open Seam, but both turnings are pressed to one side and neatened together by zigzagging, overcasting or binding with seam binding. On right side of fabric, the seam is top stitched, ususally in a heavier thread for emphasis, an even distance away from seam line.

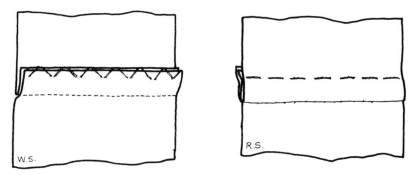

Both turnings are pressed to one side

A French seam is suitable for thin and sheer fabrics as all turnings are enclosed in the fell. It is a fairly strong seam and is easily ironed and therefore it is suitable for loose fitting underclothes and some blouses and childrens dresses. It is not a flat seam.

Directions for Making

1. Place **wrong sides** facing and balance points matching. Where seam lines are marked these should be directly on top of one another. Pin and tack along seam line.
2. Decide what the finished width of the fell should be, depending on the material used, and machine this distance away from seam line in the seam turning. Beginners may find it useful to tack this line or to mark it with tailors chalk before machining.
3. Trim to slightly **less** than the finished width of the fell away from the machining. Remove tacking.

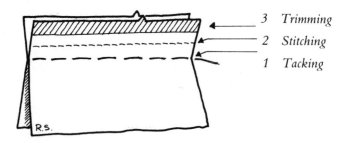

3	*Trimming*
2	*Stitching*
1	*Tacking*

4. Press seam open, using the tip of the iron.

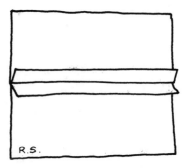

Press open

5. Fold the two right sides together and work the first line of machining to the top so that there is no groove along the top edge of the seam. The seam lines should again be on top of each other.

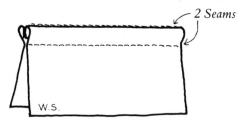

Finished French Seam

6. Pin, tack and machine along the seam line.
7. Remove tacks and press fell of seam towards back of garment.

Further points about French Seams

1. If raw edges show on right side when seam is finished this is because:-

(a) the turnings were not trimmed sufficiently after first row of stitching.
(b) the second row of stitching was not placed sufficiently low to enclose raw edges.

2. Unevenness in the seam line is caused by inaccurate stitching.
3. Puckering in the material on underside of seam is caused by inadequate preparation.

Overlaid Seam. as its name implies one portion of this seam, the upper section, is laid over the other section, the under section.

This is very useful when emphasis is required on a particular style feature such as the yoke of a dress or skirt. Very often the under section has some sort of fullness arranged in it.

Overlaid seam on a yoke

Directions for making

1. On upper section turn under seam allowance and pin and tack into position.

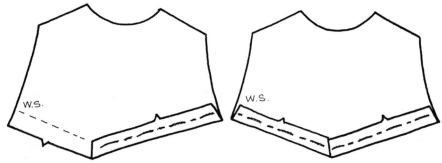

Pin and tack seam allowance under

2. If there is an acute angle in the upper section this corner should be reinforced with machine stitching just inside the seam line, on the turning, and then slashed diagonally to the corner. Similarly, for a curved upper section the seam allowance must be slashed.

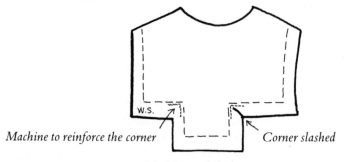

Machine to reinforce the corner   *Corner slashed*

Machine and slash at corners

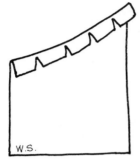

Slash curved upper section of overlaid seam

3. On under section, put in or arrange any fullness as required. Gathers are shown in the diagram but darts, pleats or tucks may be used. There may, of course, be no fullness indicated in the pattern.

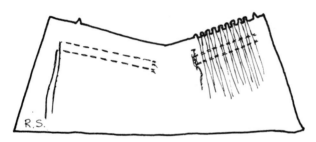

Arrange fullness on under section

4. Pin upper section over under section matching balance points and seam lines. Tack securely. Machine along folded edge of upper section.

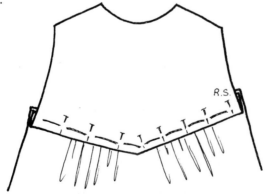

Pin, tack and machine along edge of upper section

5.   To neaten an overlaid seam, any of the methods for an open seam, except edge stitching, may be used, the turnings being neatened together for speed and because both turnings lie under the upper section. The finished seam width is usually about 1.0cm.

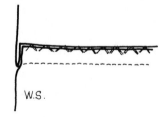

W.S.

Section of seam neatened with zigzag

A Tucked Seam is a variation of an overlaid seam, but may only be used on a straight line seam.

1.   On the upper section, twice the finished width of the tuck is added to the normal seam allowance.

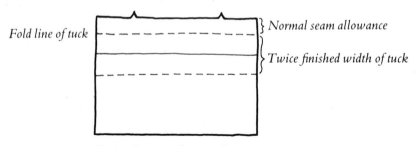

Fold line of tuck   } *Normal seam allowance*

} *Twice finished width of tuck*

Twice the normal seam allowance

2.   The upper section is folded along the fold line of tuck and tacked into position through the seam line.

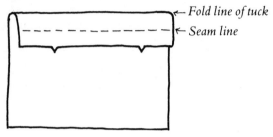

← *Fold line of tuck*

← *Seam line*

Fold and tack into position

3. The upper section is laid over the under section with seam lines matching and pinned, tacked and machined through this line. Neaten as for overlaid seam.

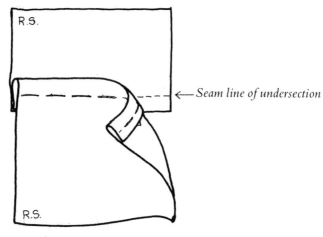

Machine stitch on right side with one-sided foot

4. Greater emphasis may be made to the tuck by laying a piping cord in the tuck at stages 1 and 2. A one sided piping foot must be used at stage 3.

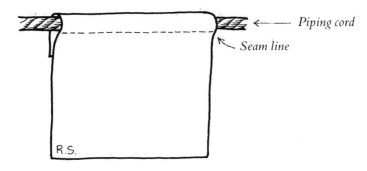

Piped tucked seam

Double Stitched Seam. This is a very strong flat seam with no raw edges showing. It works equally well in fine and thick materials and is particularly strong round curves. It has long been a popular seam for shirts and pyjamas and it is also very popular for denim jeans.

Other names for this seam are Machine fell seam and Flat fell seam.

It can be made onto either the wrong or right side, but as it is generally considered smarter when finished on the right side and with the fell towards the back of the garment, directions are given for this.

Directions for Making

1. Place wrong side of pattern pieces facing with balance points and seam lines matching. Pin, tack and machine. Remove tacks.

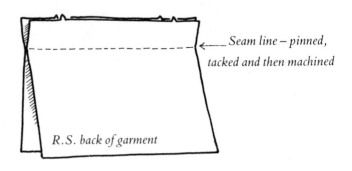

Seam line – pinned, tacked and then machined

R.S. back of garment

First stitch on right side of fabric

2. As the finished width of the fell is usually 0.5cm, trim the turning on the back of the garment to this amount. Trim the turning on the front of the garment to 1cm.

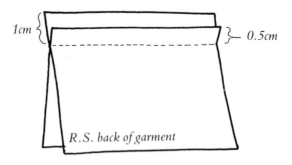

1cm   *0.5cm*

R.S. back of garment

Trim turning on back of garment

3. Fold over front turning to the back of garment and tack through all three thicknesses. Press.

Fold front raw edge over back of garment

4. Now open out seam and lay flat on ironing board, pulling the pieces well apart so that no groove lies round the first row of stitching. Press the fell to the back of the garment. Pin, tack and machine along the folded edge.

    Remove tacks and give final press.

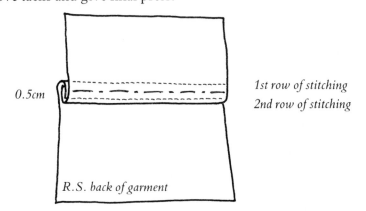

Open out seam, lay flat with right side up and press fell to back before stitching

5. Where the seam is curved the turning on the front edge is snipped up to a depth of 3mm (but no more) to allow the turnings to spread inside the fell.

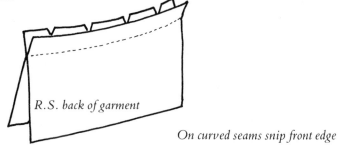

On curved seams snip front edge

9

OPENINGS

General Points

1. The strength of the opening will depend on its length, stitching and correct choice of opening.
2. A well made opening should lie quite flat when fastened.
3. The position of the opening should be considered when choosing the type as some are relatively stronger than others. The fastening to be used should also be considered.
4. When an opening is put in a seam, the seam should be stitched and neatened first, but when the opening is put into a slit, it is easier to do the opening before the seams in the garment.
5. The opening should be planned so that any fastenings can be sewn onto double material and these should be in such a position that they are easily fastened by the wearer.
6. The opening should be made on the straight grain of the fabric wherever possible. The usual exception to this is where the opening is set into a seam which may be shaped.

    The **simplest openings** are those which are planned to lie edge to edge when finished. Often they only fasten at the top. Generally, they are not so strong as other types of openings.

Hem opening in seam and without overwrap

1. The seam is stitched for the required length, but neatened for the whole length of the garment. The machine stitching must be very firmly fastened off at point A, the weak point of the opening. The seam is pressed open.

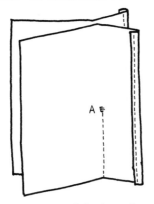

Fasten off firmly at A

2. The seam turning is slip hemmed to garment for distance XX_1 and YY_1.

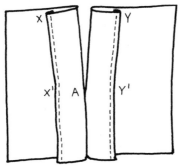

Slip hem seam turnings to garment beside opening

3. When this opening is not very long it is usually fastened with a button and loop at the top.

   This is not satisfactory when the opening has to be fairly long to permit the garment to be put on. In this case it is usual to insert a zip into the opening and there is no need to slip hem the turnings to the garment.

Faced Slit Opening. This is useful for neck openings, front or back, and wrist openings in long sleeves.

1. Cut and prepare the facing piece.

   This should be 3–5cms longer than the length of the opening and at least 8cms wide. The selvedge threads should run down the length of the facing. A pattern piece is usually provided for this in commercial patterns. On wrong side of facing, mark centre with tacks or tailors chalk. Edge stitch or finish as for seams on rest of garment on 2 long edges and 1 short edge.

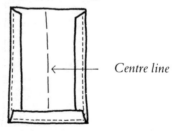

Centre line

Cut and neaten facing piece

2.   Mark position and centre line of opening on the garment. This is usually done when transferring the pattern markings from pattern to material.

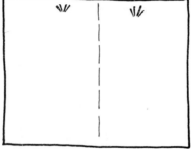

Mark centre line of opening

3.   Place right side of facing strip to right side of garment so that centre lines match. Baste into position.

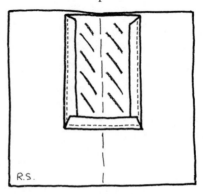

Place right sides together and baste

4. On wrong side of garment tack and machine 3mm away from centre tacking line to required length, making a blunt point at the end. This will enable the opening to be cut right to the end. Remove tacks. Cut opening right to end, taking care not to cut through stitches.

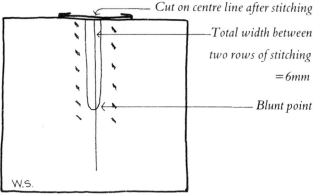

Machine round opening before cutting

5. Turn facing through to wrong side and work seam to edge of material. Tack round edge and press. As the bottom of this opening is its weakest point, the opening will be stronger if it is machined round the edge on right side as shown in diagram.

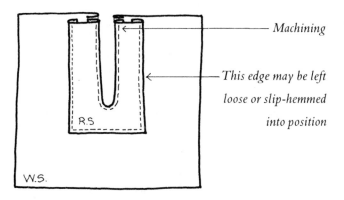

Turn facing through opening

6. The opening is usually fastened with button and loop at top edge, but it is possible to insert a zip behind the facing.

Fasten with button and loop or zipper

7. The opening can be used as a decorative finish to a neck line by starting the facing on the wrong side and finishing on the right side with decorative machine stitching.

Hem opening in seam, with overwrap.

1. For this opening an extension is cut on the seam allowance for the length of the opening.

    The seam is fixed and stitched in the usual way as far as the base of the opening.

    The seam edges are neatened as far as the opening in a method suitable for the material being used. Press seam open.

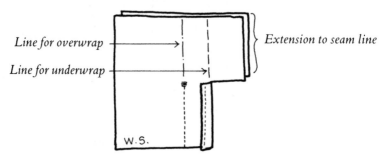

Extensions cut for length of opening

2. **For the Overwrap**. Fold turning allowance of overwrap to the wrong side. Tack and press.

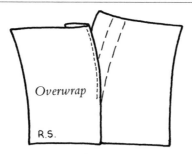

Overwrap, folded to wrong side

3. On wrong side, trim off the shaded portion of overwrap. Neaten this edge in the same way as the rest of the seam neatening.

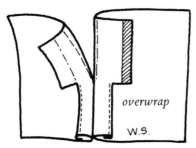

Trim and neaten overwrap

4. **For the Underwrap** snip through the turning at base of opening on underwrap and then overcast the upper edge of the seam.
   Fold turning onto the wrong side on underwrap line, pin and tack along this line. Press.
   The free edge of the underwrap is neatened in the same way as for the seam. The underwrap is now loop stitched to overwrap.

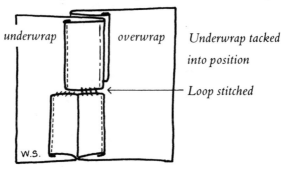

Snip underwrap and neaten cut edges

5.   On right side at the base of opening, machine through all layers to add strength to the opening. Sew on fasteners. Press fasteners are very suitable. Remove tacking.

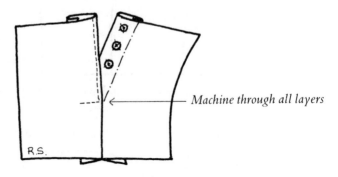

Machine stitch through all layers to strengthen base of opening

Continuous Strip Opening. This is a very useful opening to use at the wrist of shirt or blouse sleeves and also on some childrens' garments.

The opening may be put into a seam or into a slit, but the method is nearly the same.

1.   If opening is to be in a seam, stitch and neaten the seam as far as opening and trim turnings of opening to 0.5cm. If opening is to be in a slit, cut a slit in the garment to grain of the material and the exact length of opening.

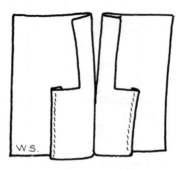

Trim seam turnings

2. Cut the strip of material on the straight of grain, twice the length of opening and twice the finished width of band plus 2 turnings, 0.5cm each, or less if a fine material. The selvedge threads should run the length of the opening.
3. Pull the edges of slit open.

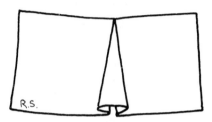

Cut edge is at top of diagram

4. With right sides facing, place edge of strip to edge of slit beginning at the right hand end. Pin and tack to within 2.5cm from base of slit. At this point the turning on the slit must taper to nothing at the base. Continue up second side of slit. Machine strip into position. Remove tacks.

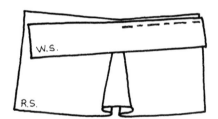 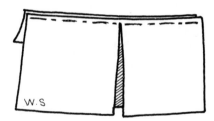

Stitch strip to edge of slit

5. On free edge of strip, make and press a turning of 0.5cm.

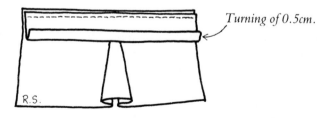

Turning of 0.5cm.

Turning on raw edge of strip

6. Take the turned edge over to the wrong side of opening and pin and tack into position just above the row of machining.

 Hem very firmly, passing the needle through each machine stitch so that no hemming stitches show on the right side.

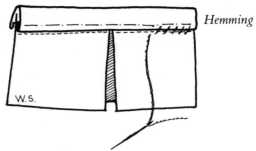

Fold over and hem to machine stitching

7. The band is now folded back and overwrap is tacked and pressed into position. Remove tacks.

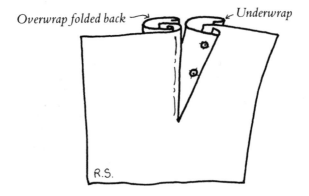

Fold, tack and press into position

8. Sew on fasteners.

Bound Opening. This is usually put into a slit. It is a very useful opening at the wrist of sleeves where very fine material is used. It is also useful for neck openings on childrens' garments.

 The method for making this opening is the same as for a continuous strip opening, but instead of using a strip of material on the straight grain, a cross-way strip or commercial bias binding is used. The resulting band is much narrower and the overlap is not usually pressed back.

It is usually fastened with a button and loop, or set into a band.

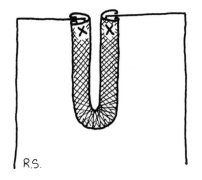

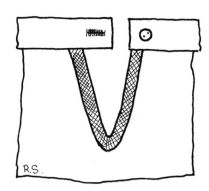

XX Position for button and loop

Bound opening set into a band

Tailored Opening. This is often used as a sleeve opening or on shirts and also at the neck of a sports blouse.
1. As shown in diagram reinforce bottom of opening and cut.

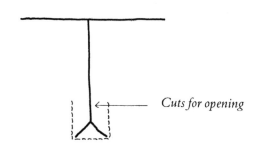

Cuts for opening

Reinforce bottom of opening and cut

2. Cut 2 strips for bands, 7cms wide on the straight of grain.
        Underwrap – length of opening + 1.5cm
        Overwrap – length of opening + 4.5cm
    With right sides facing, join bands to slashed edges of opening as shown in the diagram.
    Tack in seam allowance on the free edges of each band as shown.

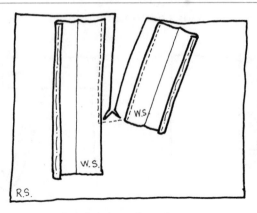

Join bands to edges of opening

3.   Fold free edges of both bands to the wrong side and lay against the
     row of stitching. Pin, tack and hem in position, taking the needle
     through each machine stitch so that the hemming does not show on
     the right side.

     Tuck end of clipped corner inside underwrap band and stitch in
     position by hand.

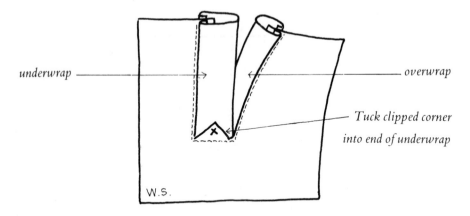

4.   On right side, turn under seam allowance at lower edge and pin
     into position through all layers. Tack and machine as shown.
     Remove tacks.

     On thicker materials the inside of the overwrap may be cut away
     below the base of the opening. The end of the overwrap is
     sometimes arranged in a point.

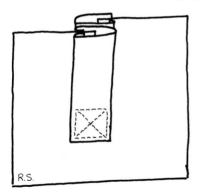

Machine through all layers

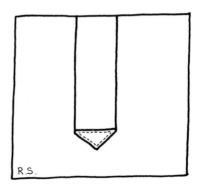

Alternative finish to overwrap

10

HEMS

This is one of the easiest ways of finishing the outer edges of garments and articles. It may be very narrow, machine or hand sewn, or much wider according to the style and position of the hem. Except on very thick materials, a hem is turned twice so that no raw edges show.

Simple Hems

Rolled Hems are used on very thin fabrics. As very little turning is used on this hem, the edge is trimmed to a little beyond the required finished length or size.

No pinning or tacking is required, the hem being rolled between the fingers of the left hand whilst it is oversewn with the right hand, taking the needle through the upper layers of the rolled hem only, so there will be no stitching visible on the right side.

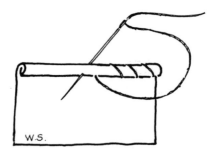

Hand stitching a rolled hem

Narrow Machined Hems are very useful for the edges of a frill or on a very full skirt as there is so little weight to them. Allow 1cm turning allowance.

1. Turn 0.6cm to wrong side, tack and machine close to the fold. Trim excess fabric away.

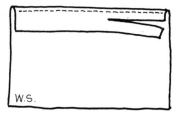

First line of stitching

2. Turn a second time to the wrong side to a depth of 0.4cms. The first row of machining is visible at edge of hem. Tack and then machine on this first line of machining. Only one line of machining will be seen on the right side.

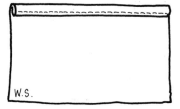

Machine a second line of stitching

Wider Hems

Straight hems. Decide on the finished width of the hem and add 1cm for turnings. Trim the hem allowance to this amount.

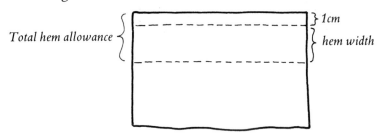

Hem width plus 1cm

1. Turn over 1cm to the wrong side of the fabric. Press into position.

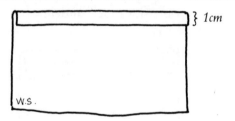

Turn up 1cm

2. Turn over the hem a second time for the amount planned. Pin and tack into position.

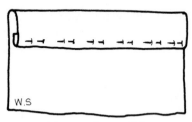

Turn up hem width

3. This lower edge may now be secured with permanent stitching such as machining, hemming, slip-hemming or an embroidery stitch as appropriate.

Treatment of corners in flat articles

It frequently happens that hems overlap at the corners of flat articles. To avoid having a thick lump at such a corner, bulk may be removed by cutting away surplus material or by mitreing the corner.

(a)   Cutting away surplus material

1. Prepare hems on longer side as just described for straight hems, but stop the tacking before the position for the other hem is reached.

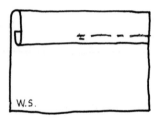

Leave untacked near corner

2. Crease, or mark in the turnings for the other hem.

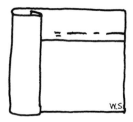

Mark for other hem

3. Cut away the shaded portion.

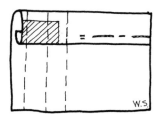

Remove surplus fabric

4. Refold the second hem and tack into position. Hold down hem with chosen stitch, oversewing the corner very firmly.

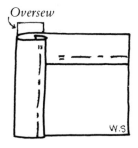

Work both hems and oversew corner

(b) **Mitreing the corner** gives a much more professional finish and is not really difficult, but great accuracy is called for.

1. Crease and press in the turnings on both hems taking great care that they are both exactly the same width. Crease in the diagonal.

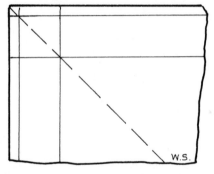

Mark both hems exactly

2. Now fold right sides together along the diagonal.
    The creases of the two hems should be exactly on top of one
    another.
    Pin together.

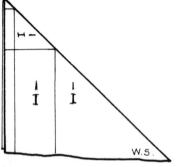

Fold exactly diagonally

3. From the point A, which will be the finished corner, mark with
    tailors' chalk down the finished hem width to B, forming a square
    A, A_1, B, B_1. Stitch very accurately from A to B_1. If the hem width
    is not very wide, backstitch may be used, otherwise machine.
    On no account stitch into what is to be the turning of the hem.
    Trim off the two triangles, i.e. the shaded triangle and the solid
    triangle.

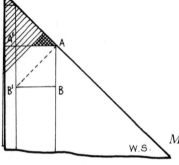

Measure, mark, stitch and trim

4. Now fold hems into original position, pushing the point A to its finished position. A pin may be needed to ease the corner out to a good shape. The line of stitching, A B_1, will now form a diagonal in the corner of the hems.

Tack hems into position and finish with an appropriate stitch.

When using a fabric such as evenweave linen, which is the same on both sides of the fabric, this method of mitreing a corner can successfully be used on the right side.

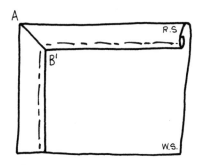

A neatly mitred corner

Levelling a dress hem

1. A garment which has any 'bias' in its style needs to be hung on a clothes hanger for at least a week before the hem is levelled. This is so that those parts which are on the bias can be stretched to their full extent by the weight of the fabric.

2. Put garment on the wearer and do up any fastenings including belt. The model should be wearing appropriate shoes.

3. The wearer should stand naturally straight with arms by side and head held level. It is very important that the wearer should maintain this stance during the levelling process as any movement will alter the position of the garment. A hem can be successfully levelled when the wearer is standing on the floor but it is sometimes more convenient to stand on a table whose surface is protected with paper.

4. Decide on the finished position of hem and use a metre stick or skirt marker to measure this distance from the floor.

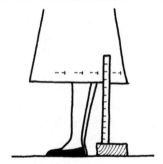

Measuring hem height with a skirt marker

5. Keep the measuring aid as close to the garment as possible and go around the wearer putting pins at regular intervals to mark the distance from the floor. Try to disarrange the folds of the skirt as little as possible.
6. Remove the garment and fold turning to the wrong side along the line of pins. Tack along this edge and pin up the surplus material.

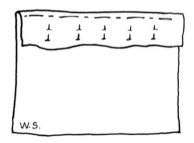

Fold along line of pins

7. Try on garment again to check that hem is level.
8. How the hem is finished depends on the garment and the material. For cotton and other similar light weight materials the hem may be turned twice but for woollens and heavier type fabrics this would cause a ridge on the right side. For these types of fabrics it is usual to turn the hem only once and neaten the raw edge in some way.
    For adult garments the finished hem width is approximately 3cm, but for childrens garments a rather deeper hem may be used so that it may be let down at a later date. In no case should the hem dominate the garment but it should be as inconspicuous as possible.

9. **For cotton type fabrics**

(a)   The hem allowance must be corrected to an even width all the way around the hem, i.e. finished hem width plus turning allowance.

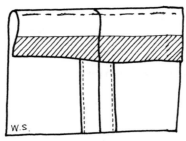

Trim away shaded portion

(b)   Fold under the turning allowance and tack. A firm finish is obtained if this fold is edge-stitched. Fold the hem down making sure that the seam lines match.

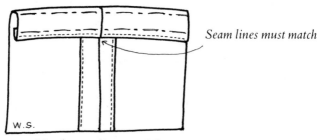

Seam lines must match

Match seam lines carefully

(c)   On straight or slightly flared garments, the hem will lie flat, but on very flared garments the hem will have to be pleated to make it lie flat.

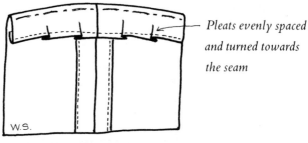

Pleats evenly spaced and turned towards the seam

Pin pleats first and then stitch

(d)   On cotton type materials the hem is usually slip-hemmed.

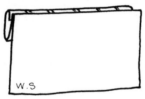

Slip-hemming

10.   **For woollen and heavier materials**

The hem allowance is corrected to the final width of the hem and any fullness in the hem allowance is dealt with either by pleating as described for cotton type fabrics or by easing or gathers. A single row of machine gathers is worked in each section of the skirt hem and pulled up so that the hem lies flat.

On many fabrics, particularly wool or wool mixtures, this fullness can be entirely shrunk away by using a hot iron and a damp cloth on the areas to be shrunk.

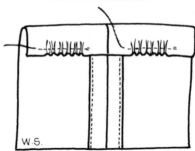

Gather each section separately

(a)   The lower edge of the skirt is then neatened by the method used for any open seams in the garment, e.g. overcasting, binding, zigzagging or 3-step zigzag.

(b)   On this type of fabric the hem is best held down by catch stitch between the hem and the garment.

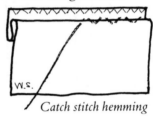

Catch stitch hemming

(c) If choosing to use seam binding to neaten the edge of the hem, it may be put on as a binding as when neatening a seam edge, or alternatively by a flat method.

Flat method. The seam binding is machined to the seam allowance with wrong side of seam binding to right side of seam allowance.

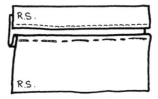

Machine on seam binding

(d) The hem is now folded into position and the lower edge is caught down very loosely.

It is particularly important when using either method with seam binding, that the final stitching is kept fairly loose as too tight a stitch will cause a ridge on the right side. (Too loose a stitch will not hold the hem for very long!)

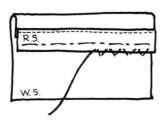

Catch binding down very loosely

Blind Hemming

If there is a blind hem selector on your machine it is appropriate to use this on any type of fabric.

'Blind' stitch consists of four or five straight stitches and then one zigzag.

Blind stitch

It is the zigzag part of the combined stitch that just goes into the upper part of the garment.

The hem is prepared in the normal way, folded back as shown and held with the bulk of the work on the left hand side of the machine.

Set selector knob at required position as described in the instruction booklet provided with your machine.

Sometimes a hemming plate is also provided with the machine. This is a useful aid (but not essential) to guiding the hem so that the zigzag stitch takes just the correct amount of bite into the folded edge – too little and the hem will not be held down, too much and the hem is far from invisible.

Hem folded back　　　　　*blind-stitched*

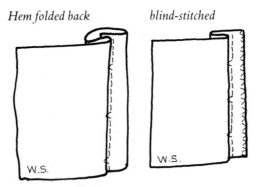

Zigzag catching one thread only of folded edge

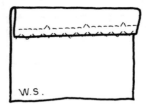

Finished hem on wrong side

False Hem

Sometimes when the hem has been levelled, there is very little material left with which to make a hem. This may also happen when a garment is being lengthened. When this happens an extra strip of fabric has to be used to form the hem. For straight skirts a straight piece of fabric may be used, but for flared garments it is best to use material cut on the cross. It is possible to buy ready prepared fabric for this purpose (3cm wide bias binding).

When putting a false hem on thick material, a thinner material of toning colour is often used as this reduces bulk.

1. Level hem in usual way and correct hem allowance to widest possible, probably only 1 to 2cms.
2. Fold over this allowance on hem line. Tack and press into position.

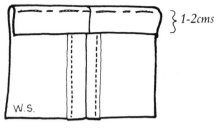

Fold hem over

3. The strip for the false hem is placed to the edge of the hem allowance, then tacked into place and then machined. Remove tacks.

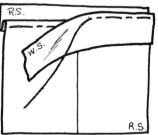

Strip for false hem

Tack false hem in place

4. The hem is folded back to the wrong side and the false hem strip is pressed down. The lower edge is turned under and tacked into position. Final stitching used to hold the hem down depends on the fabric, e.g. slip-hemming for cotton types, blind hemming for heavier materials.

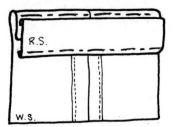

False hem on wrong side

11

CUTTING AND JOINING CROSSWAY STRIPS

The true cross of the material is found when the material is folded so that the warp threads lie along the weft threads. This is perhaps easiest to understand when working with a square of material.

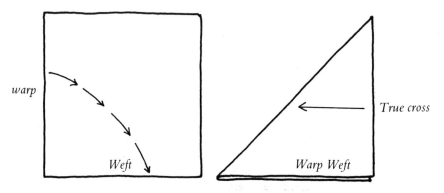

Square folded diagonally to show true cross

However this is not really economical and it is better to get used to working from irregular shaped pieces of material.

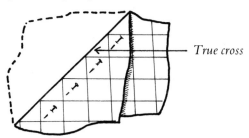

True Cross on irregular shaped fabric

111

Pin two layers together a little way from the fold. Slit through the fold.

Two layers pinned together

To cut strips, measure the width of the strip required at right angles to cut edge. Mark width with tailors chalk or faint pencil dots. Pins make cutting the strips difficult. Cut very carefully along the marked line.

To join Crossway Strips. The joins should always be on the selvedge thread.

1.   Straighten ends of all the strips to selvedge thread.

Straighten ends of strips

2.   Place 2 selvedge edges together right sides facing so that the strip will be in a straight line when the join is stitched and pressed open. The acutely pointed ends of the strip should project.
     Pin, tack and machine exactly where the strips cross.

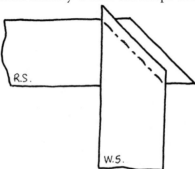

Begin stitching exactly where strips cross with right sides together.

3. Remove tacks and press the seam open. Trim off the points which project beyond the strip.

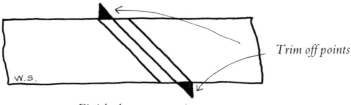

Finished crossway strip

When large quantities of cross way strips are required it is tedious to fix and stitch perhaps some 50 joins.

1. Decide how wide the strip is required to be.
2. From left over fabric cut as long and as wide a rectangle as possible, taking great care to cut to the straight grain.
    Trim off shaded portion of rectangle.

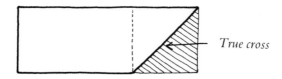

Large rectangle of left over fabric

3. On long edge, measure off the required width of the strip from the point.

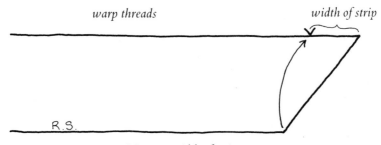

Measure width of strip

4. With right sides facing, pin shorter edge to this mark and continue pinning the two edges for the whole length of the rectangle. Tack and then machine.

Join straight, long edges

The resultant seam will appear to twist round the band thus:-

The seam twists round

5.   Slip ruler through the band. Starting from the marked width of strip, cut continuously at this depth in *single* fabric turning the band round the ruler.

Cut single fabric continuously

6.   When the whole band has been cut, it will be found that all the joins in the strip are on the straight grain and can be pressed open and the points trimmed off.

    Although this method may seem difficult at first glance, it can save considerable time once the technique is mastered.

12

USE OF CROSSWAY STRIPS
ON EDGES OF FABRIC

Binding

As well as neatening the edge of the fabric, binding adds a certain amount of strength to the edge. It also adds decoration especially if a contrasting fabric is used for the binding.

From the diagram it can be seen that there are five layers of material on a bound edge. It is therefore only suitable to use on fine and some medium weight fabrics.

The usual finished width of a binding is about 0.5cms.

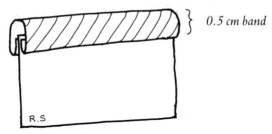

0.5 cm band

R.S

1. Decide upon the finished width of the binding and cut the crossway strips 4 times this width. Join as necessary. Trim the edge of the garment down to the seam line, making sure that there is a good line.
2. Press cross way strip in half along its length with wrong sides facing.

R.S.

Folded cross way strip

115

3.   Open out and press each raw edge to centre fold and press in place.

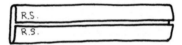

Press raw edges to centre fold

4.   Open out one edge of the cross way strip and with right sides facing, place the strip to the trimmed edge of garment fabric. The crossway strip should be **slightly** stretched. Pin, tack and machine along the crease of the crossway strip and remove tacks.

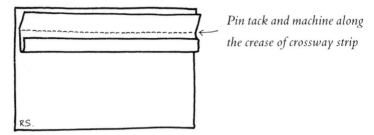

Pin tack and machine along the crease of crossway strip

5.   For curved or pointed edges, the crossway strip must be stretched, eased or pleated.

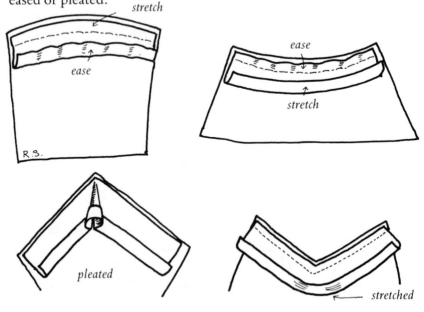

Stretched, eased or pleated cross way strips

6. Fold the crossway strip to the wrong side and lay the folded edge of the strip to the row of machining.

    Pin and tack and strip into position.

    The folded edge of the strip is held in place with hemming, the needle being taken through each machine stitch so that no stitches show on the right side.

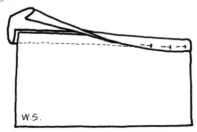

W.S.

Fold over to wrong side

7. **Final join:** When crossway strips are being used round an armhole.

    (i)   Pin and tack crossway strip to right side as before until the beginning of the strip is almost reached.

    (ii)   On the beginning of the strip, mark in the turning allowance for the join with a pin.

    (iii) Overlap the second end and mark the position of the join with a pin. Mark in turning allowance for join beyond this mark and trim off excess fabric taking care to cut to straight of grain.

    (iv)   The strips may now be joined in the usual way and should fit accurately around the armhole.

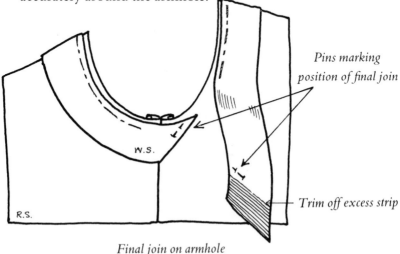

Pins marking position of final join

W.S.

R.S.

Trim off excess strip

Final join on armhole

8.   Trim off shaded portion and complete tacking over the join.

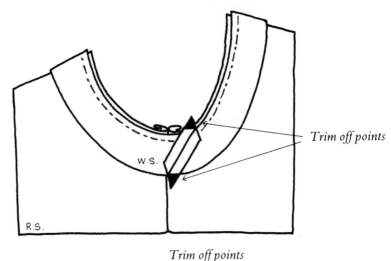

Trim off points

9.   Finish binding in the usual way.

For very narrow binding

This is particularly effective on babies' clothing and it also looks well on pure silk.

The strip should not be cut less than 1.75cms.

1.   Trim edge to be bound, to seam line.
2.   The cross-way strip should lie flat and **not** be pressed into four.
   Place strip to the edge of the fabric with right sides facing.
   Pin, tack and stitch 2mm from cut edge. If using very fine fabric, trim 2mm from lower edge of the crossway strip.

Place strip to edge of fabric

3. Fold the lower edge of crossway strip up to the row of stitching and press into position.

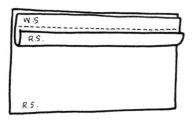

Fold other edge to stitching

4. Bring this fold over to the machining on the wrong side of the garment edge and pin and tack into position. Hem through machining as before. Because there is an extra layer in this method it is only suitable for very fine fabrics.

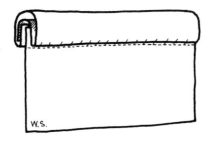

Fold over and hem to machining

Piping

This is a method of decorating edges and seams. It is a fold of crossway strip which protrudes from the edge or seam and may or may not contain a cord. Caution must be exercised if using cord in a garment which is to be washed frequently as the cord could shrink. Either cotton cord must be pre-shrunk or nylon or terylene should be used.

Contrast in colour, texture and pattern may be introduced for added decoration.

Method without cord

1. Cut and join sufficient crossway strips 2.5cm wide.
2. With wrong sides facing, fold crossway strip in half and tack together at required depth of piping from folded edge.

Fold cross way strip

3. Place tacking line of piping on seam line of edge or seam. Note that all raw edges are on the same side of the seam line. Pin and tack through the seam line.

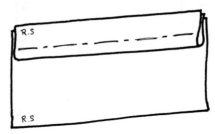

Pin tacking line to seam line

4. Now place facing or otherside of seam on top of the piping so that the right sides are facing and the seam lines are on top of one another.

    Pin tack and machine through this line. Remove tacks. Trim the turning to an even depth of 0.5cm.

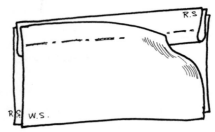

Pin second seam line to other two stitching lines

For a piped edge

The facing is turned over to the wrong side so that the piping protrudes from the edge. Laundering the garment is much easier if the top edge is machined close to the edge.

The lower edge may be fixed down with slip hemming or edge stitched and left free as for a facing.

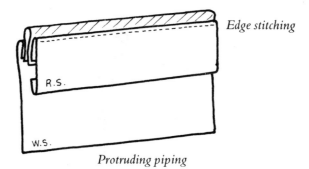

Edge stitching

Protruding piping

For a seam

The turnings are pressed to one side and neatened together by zigzagging or overcasting.

Edges neatened together

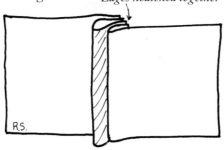

Press turnings to one side

Piping with a cord

1. Cut strip as before, but if the cord is very thick, the strip must be cut wider to allow the cord to pass through the piping.
2. Fold the strip round the cord and tack into position.

Strip folded round cord

3. For extra firmness, the tacked line is machined. Remove tacks.
    Proceed as for method without cord, *but* in step 3., pin tack and *machine* through seamline, machining as close as possible to the cord. (a piping foot is necessary for this) and at step 4., turn work so that the line of machining in step 3 is visible and machine exactly through this line.

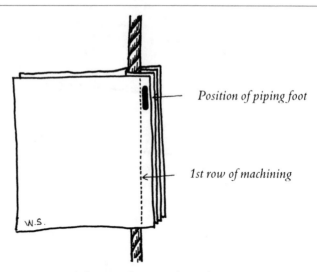

Position of piping foot

1st row of machining

One sided piping foot must be used

Cross Way Facings are a useful finish for armholes, necklines, collars, hems etc. Unlike bindings, they are only visible from one side but this may be either the wrong or the right side if a decorative finish is required. Inasmuch as there is less strain on a narrow turning, a facing gives a much stronger finish to the edge than a binding does.

The strips should be cut to the finished width of the facings plus the width of two turnings.

For straight edges – e.g. flat articles, pocket tops etc.
1. Crease and press in the turnings to the wrong side of the facing strip.

Press turnings

2. With right sides facing, place facing strip to edge so that one folded edge of the facing lies along the seam line of the edge that is to be faced.
   Fold back the turning and pin, tack and machine along this line. Remove tacks.
   Trim turnings to an even width of 0.5cms.

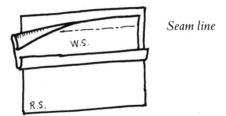

Place fold of facing strip to seam line of fabric

3. Turn the facing to the wrong side and work the seam right up to the top edge. Tack along this edge. As crossway facings are usually no wider than 1.5cms, extra firmness is achieved if the top edge is machined.

   The lower edge is tacked into position and is machined or if a less visible finish is required, slip-hemming is used.

Facing in place on wrong side of garment piece

For curved edges

As for binding, the edges of the facing should be stretched or eased according to whether the edge is convex or concave. The turnings must also be snipped at outer edges to allow the turnings to lie properly. If a wider facing is required it is more practical to use a shaped facing. A crossway facing of perhaps 3cm will tend to roll back to the outside and if stitched down at this width, could look rather clumsy.

Concave	Convex

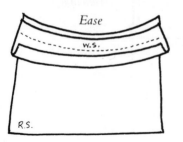

Ease facing on concave curve

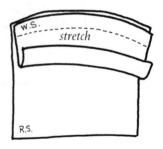

Stretch facing on convex curve

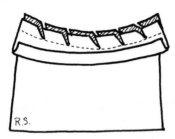

*Turnings are clipped diagonally
so they may spread when
facing is turned to the other side.
Do not cut into machine stitching.*

*Small 'V' shaped pieces are removed
from the turnings so that they will lie
flat when the facing is turned to the
other side. Do not cut into
machine stitching.*

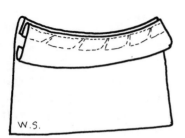

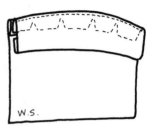

Position of clipped turnings on inside of curves are shown by the faint line

13

OTHER EDGE FINISHES

For a **Straight Edge** finish, a straight strip of material may be used to face the edge just as well as a crossway strip. The method is identical except that the strip is cut accurately to the straight grain. Whichever method is used, i.e. straight of crossway, depends largely on the amount of material available as a straight strip cuts into less material than a crossway strip. The choice of method can also be affected if the finish is to be decorative.

1. Where the edge is shaped the strip is cut to the same shape at the outer edge as the edge to be faced.
2. With right sides facing, the strip is matched to the shaped edge and pinned, tacked and machined along the seam line.
   There must be no irregularities in the machining as this will spoil the finished line of the facing.
3. The turnings are trimmed to 0.5cm and any curves or corners are snipped, being careful not to cut the machining, to allow the turnings to spread and lie flat.

Strip cut to same shape

4. The facing is turned to the wrong side of the edge and the seam is worked to the top. Tack and machine along this edge.
   The lower edge of the facing may be neatened according to the fabric and left free or it may be slip hemmed into position.

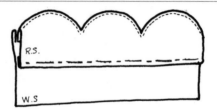

Facing turned to wrong side and edge machined

5. If the facing is finished onto the right side as part of the decoration, this lower edge may be held in position with an embroidery stitch.

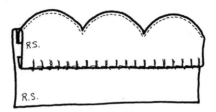

Decorative embroidered edge to facing

For a **Curved Edge,** a crossway facing may only be used if the finish is to be a narrow one.

A Shaped Facing must be used for a wider finish on a curved edge.

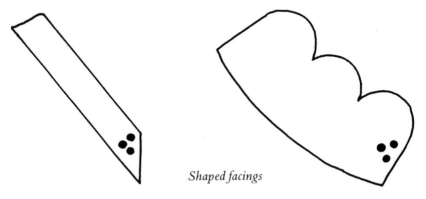

Shaped facings

1. The facing must be cut exactly to the same shape as the edge that is to be faced. If the outer edge is very shaped, e.g. scalloped, it is usual for the inner edge to be cut to a more simple shape. In a commercial pattern, pattern pieces for facings are supplied.

2. Make any joins that are necessary in the facing, e.g. shoulder seams
    on a neck facing. Check that the corresponding seams are stitched
    and neatened in the main part of the garment. This is because it is
    very much stronger to have the facings going across the seams than
    to face the edges and then join the pieces together.

3. If a zip is planned as a neck fastening, this should be inserted next.

4. With right sides together, the facing is placed round the neck,
    matching balance points and seam lines. The seams of the facing
    should lie directly over the seams of the bodice.

    Pin, tack and machine **very accurately** on the seam line.

Neck facing

5. Remove tacks and trim turnings to 0.5cm. Snip curves and corners
    so that turnings will lie flat.

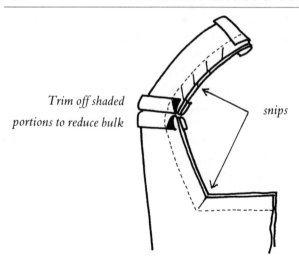

Trim off shaded portions to reduce bulk

snips

Trim turnings and snip corners

6.   Understitching gives a professional finish to a faced edge as it holds the seam firmly in position and prevents it rolling to the outside. The facing is lifted up preparatory to turning to the wrong side of the garment and trimmed and snipped turnings are tacked and machined to it. The facing is turned to the inside working the first row of machining seam to the top edge. The understitching is not visible from the right side.

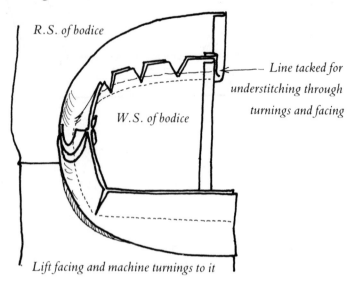

R.S. of bodice

Line tacked for understitching through turnings and facing

W.S. of bodice

Lift facing and machine turnings to it

7. The lower edge of the facing is neatened according to the fabric, e.g. edge-stitching or zigzagging. It is usual for facings finished on the wrong side to be stitched in place at the seams only at the lower edge of the facing.

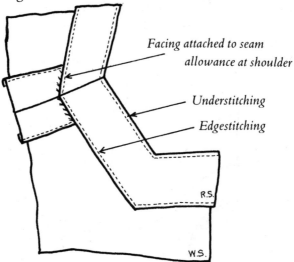

Facing attached to seam allowance at shoulder

Understitching

Edgestitching

R.S.

W.S.

Anchor facings at seams only

All – in – One Facings

Sometimes the shoulder seam of a sleeveless garment is so narrow that the armhole and neck facings are cut in one.

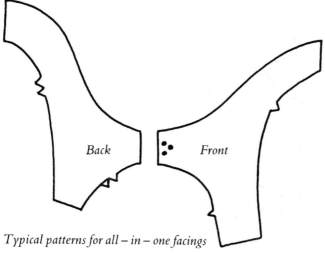

Back

Front

Typical patterns for all – in – one facings

1. The shoulder seams of the garment and facings are made and
    pressed open. On no account should the side seams be worked and
    either the centre front or centre back seam should be left open for
    its entire length. With right sides facing, the balance points and
    seam lines of the facing and garment are matched.
    The seam lines at the neck edge and both armhole edges are pinned,
    tacked and then stitched.
    Remove tacks. Trim and snip turnings.

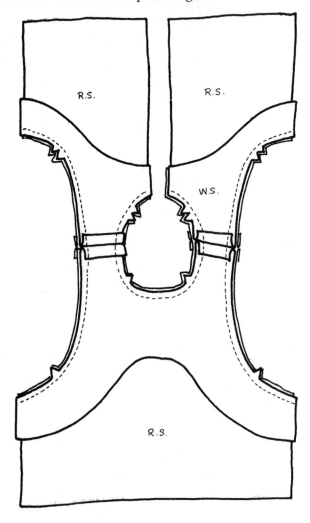

All – in – one neck facings

2. Now take each side of the back bodice and push it between the facing and the garment, through the shoulder section. Work seams at neck and armholes to the outer edge. Tack and press.

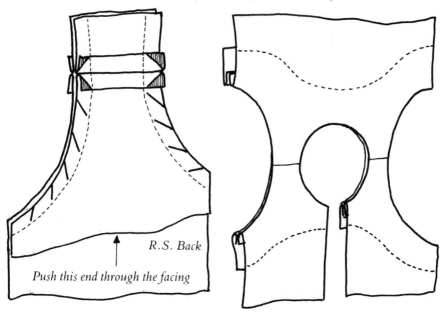

How to turn to right side

3. For the side seam, the facing is lifted and the seam line is extended through the facing.

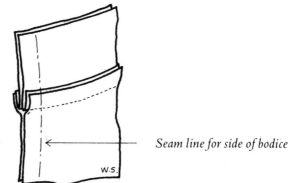

Seam line for side of bodice

Seam line extended through facing

4. Neaten the edges of the seam and free edge of the facing according to the fabric used. Fold facing to wrong side and attach to the garment at the seam.

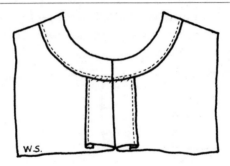

Neatly finished neck facing

Many facings look much smarter and have a more professional finish if an interfacing is used in conjunction with them.

Interfacings have not been used in any of the methods described as this would perhaps have confused the reader.

A section on interfacings is included later in the book and the general rules therein can then be applied to facings.

Frills

Frills are usually gathered but fullness may be controlled by tiny pleats. Frills should always be cut with the selvedge or warp threads running down the frill, i.e. the shorter length.

1. Make a hem on the frill according to the depth of the frill e.g. narrow machined hem for usual frill.

    If the frill is a long one, divide it into equal sections of not more than 50cms each. This is for convenience when pulling up the gathers as the gathering threads may break if pulled over a long section.

2. Put in 2 rows of gathers either by hand or by machine in each section, 1 row on the seam line and the second in the seam allowance.

3. Divide edge to which the frill is to be attached into the same number of sections as the frill.

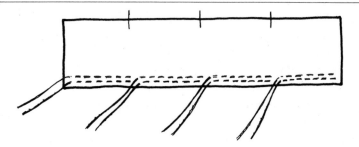

4 sections in a flat article

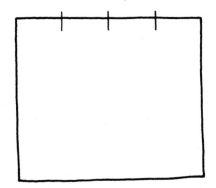

8 sections in a round garment

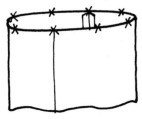

Divide up length of frill

4.   Matching each section division, place the right side of the frill to the right side of the garment. Pin at each section division. Working one section at a time, pull up the gathers until the frill is the correct size and secure gathering threads around pin. Arrange the gathers evenly. Pin and tack through the seam line.

5.   When the gathers in all sections are tacked, machine the complete length of the frill on the seam line.
Remove tacks.

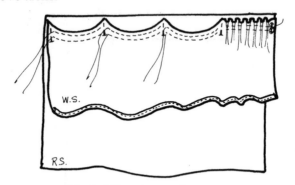

Match frill sections to those on garment
and pull up gathers.   Tack and stitch.

6.   There are two methods of neatening the join of the frill to a garment.
(a)   A second row of machining is worked 0.5cm away from the first row, in the seam allowance.
Trim the seam allowance close to the second row of machining. The raw edges may then be overcast, zigzagged or bound.

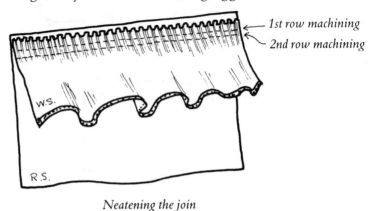

Neatening the join

(b)   The seam allowance of the frill only is trimmed to 4mm.

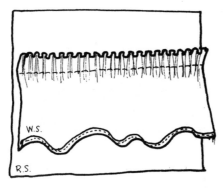

Trim frill only

The turning on the garment is trimmed to 1.2cm and then turned to form a hem over the gathered edge of the frill. This is tacked into position and may then be hemmed or machined. Remove tacks.

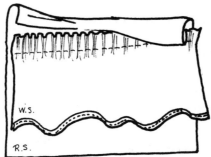

Hem over frill edge

7.   Any gathering threads which are visible from either side should be removed.

Lace Finish

Lace for edges is obtainable in a variety of widths and it is usually made of cotton or nylon thread. Hand made lace in linen thread is still made in some countries but it is extremely expensive.

Good quality machine made lace should have a firm, well finished edge that will give good wear. The straight edge of the lace, called the footside in hand made lace, often has a very fine thread woven into it which can be pulled easily. This can be used to gather up the lace if a full effect is required.

Attaching lace by hand

(a)   For very fine fabric, the lace is whipped to the hem as it is rolled between the fingers.

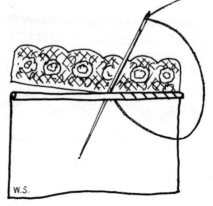

For very fine fabric

(b)   Only suitable for firm, fine materials. The straight edge of the lace is placed to the turning allowance line on the right side of fabric and tacked in place.

A very firm satin stitch in matching thread is used to cover the footside of the lace.

Remove tacks and trim away the excess material on the wrong side.

For firm, fine fabric

Attaching lace by Machine

(a)   The second method just described may be used if a zigzag machine is available. The stitch width control should be set at $1\frac{1}{2} - 2$ and the stitch length a very small one. This will result in a satin stitch effect which is much quicker to do than by hand.

(b)   With a narrow hem – this is very suitable for the edge of a frill.
1.   Trim hem allowance to 1cm.
2.   Turn over 0.6cm to the wrong side, tack and machine close to the fold. Trim away excess of the material.

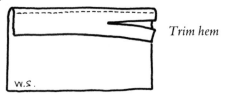

Trim hem

3.   Turn a second turning to the wrong side and tack into position. From the right side, tack lace in position so that the edge of the lace just comes below the tacking stitches holding the hem in position. Tack.

Machine at the footside of the lace and this will hold the hem in place, as well as attaching the lace.

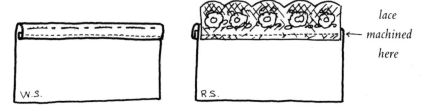

lace
machined here

Machining holds lace and hem

Joins in lace

It is sometimes necessary to join lace. This is best done by a flat seam and if possible so that the join is concealed by the pattern of the lace.

The lace is overlapped so that the pattern matches.

Using a matching sewing thread, work a row of tiny running stitches through both layers following the outline of the pattern.

Work a very fine satin stitch over the running stitch. Trim away excess lace from both sides.

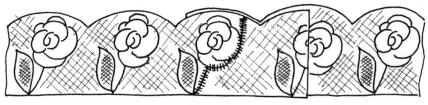

Joining Lace

14

INTERFACINGS

Types of Interfacing

All interfacings must have the following properties
  (1) Be washable
  (2) Be easy to handle
  (3) Be reasonably inexpensive
  (4) Be of such a thickness that it will not add bulk to the fabric it is being used with.
Basically there are 2 main types: woven, and non-woven or bonded.

Woven

These are generally made from cotton and some of the more expensive canvases for coat interfacings are made from linen.
  Cotton interfacings – Organdie, lawn,
  Linen interfacings – Collar Canvas, Holland, Tailors Linen

Non Woven or Bonded

These are usually made from man-made fibres and look somewhat like blotting paper in appearance. There are many trade names for this type of interfacing and they can be bought in a variety of widths and weights and in black and white.

Many also have a shiny surface on one side which melts with the moderate heat from an iron and fuses the interfacing to the material, or to the iron if one inadvertantly presses the shiny side. Rather difficult to remove from the iron so beware!

There is also a bonded interfacing which has the appearance of medium weight net and has quite a bit of stretch to it. This is specially for use with jersey knit fabrics.

Why and When to Use

Interfacing is used whenever the following are required.
(a)   Crispness, as on collar and cuffs.
(b)   Strength, as in belts and where buttonholes are to be worked.
(c)   Permanent shaping, as in jacket collars and lapels.

What Kind to Use

The fabric and design of the garment will dictate the weight of interfacing to use. Generally, the heavier the fabric, the heavier the interfacing that is used, but always the interfacing must be lighter in weight than the fabric in which it is being used.

If the garment fabric is a light colour, a white interfacing should be chosen, while a black should be chosen for a black or dark coloured fabric.

Woven versus non woven

For blouses and dresses, there is little to choose between the two sorts, provided the correct weight is chosen.

For coats and jackets, which require collar and lapels to be moulded into shape, non woven interfacings do not 'give' as do woven ones and therefore tend not to give quite the desired effect.

Sew-on versus Iron-on

Generally iron-on interfacings are easier for beginners to use but remember they are best kept for:-
(a)   Small areas such as collars and cuffs as they may not fuse evenly to large areas.
(b)   Firm materials as the adhesive can damage the appearance of some soft fabrics.

Cutting Interfacings

Interfacings are cut exactly the same shape as the shape they are to interface. A pattern is usually provided in commercial patterns.

Woven interfacings must have exactly the same grain as the shape they are interfacing, otherwise the two grains will pull against one another and cause puckering. Bonded interfacings can be cut in any direction.

To put in Interfacing

1. Baste interfacings in position while garment is still in flat sections.
2. Lay the piece to be interfaced on a flat surface, wrong side uppermost.
3. Lay on the interfacing, and if using woven interfacing, match the grains of the two fabrics very carefully.
   Pin securely and diagonally baste into position while still flat on the table. Remove pins. On sharp corners trim away the interfacing so that the seam line on the fabric of the garment is just visible.

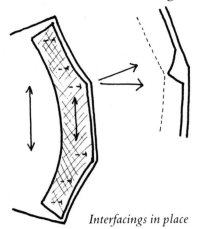

Interfacing trimmed away

Interfacings in place

Where the edge of the interfacing goes to a fold line, this edge must be caught down after the interfacing has been basted into position. This is to prevent the interfacing rolling up during laundering.

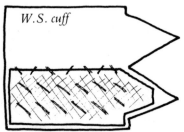

W.S. cuff

Interfacing catch stitched to fold line of cuff

4. Generally, the interfacing is best placed next to the layer of the garment which is going to be uppermost. This is so that the interfacing will make a shield over the turnings.

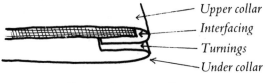

- Upper collar
- Interfacing
- Turnings
- Under collar

Section through a collar

However, with iron-on interfacings, the nature of the material may be so altered, that if this interfacing really must be used, it is better to fuse it to the under collar.

Layering Turnings – sometimes called grading seams

This is necessary on thick materials and wherever interfacing is used to reduce bulk in the seams at the edges of the garment.

(a) Remove tacks and press sections machined.
(b) Trim interfacing turnings almost to machining
(c) Trim next turning to 3mm
(d) Trim last turning to 6mm
(e) Snip any corners or curves.

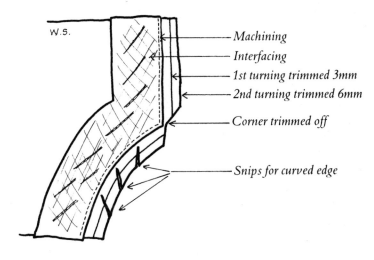

W.S.

- Machining
- Interfacing
- 1st turning trimmed 3mm
- 2nd turning trimmed 6mm
- Corner trimmed off
- Snips for curved edge

Layered turnings

5.   Once all the interfacings are in position so that they will not move
     out of position whilst working, the garment may be made up in the
     usual way.

     N.B. Leave diagonal basting tacks in position until final press to
     avoid any risk of the interfacing slipping out of position, but take
     care not to press over these tacks as this may mark the fabric.

15

COLLARS

Collars fall into two main types; those which lie flat around the neck and those which stand up in at least one portion of the neck.

Flat Styles

These are often known as Peter Pan collars. The neck edge of the collar is the same as the neck of the garment, but the outer edge of the collar may be plain or decorative. The collar may be narrow or wide.

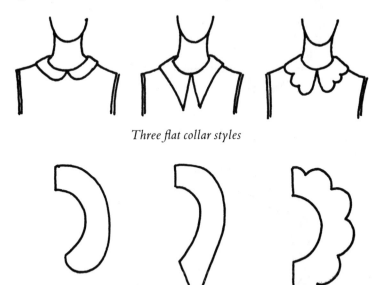

Three flat collar styles

Three half-collar patterns

To make the collar

1.   Baste interfacing to the wrong side of the upper collar.

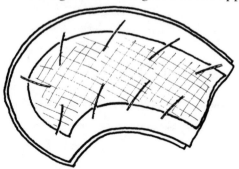

Basting on under collar

2.   With right sides together, place collar facing to the upper collar and interfacing. Pin, tack and machine on the seam line of the collar. Remove tacks.

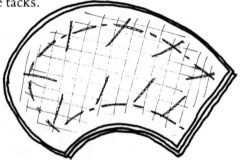

Pin, tack and machine collar

3.   Layer turnings (the widest part being 6mm). Snip out small triangles of material around the curve.

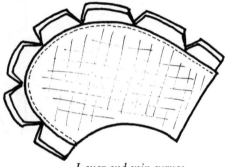

Layer and snip curves

4. Turn the collar to the right side, working the seam so that it is very slightly to the underside of the collar. Pin and tack the outer edge of the collar.

Baste through the middle of the collar to keep it flat whilst attaching it to the collar.

If the collar is to be top stitched at the outer edge, it may be done at this stage if wished. Press collar.

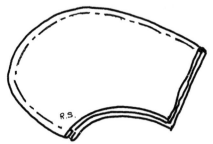

Collar turned to right side

To attach the collar

1. Any seams and darts that go into the neckline must be finished.
2. Mark centre back of the bodice and the collar if not already done.
3. Place the collar on the right side of the bodice, matching centre back, centre front and any balance points.

Pin and tack through seam line.

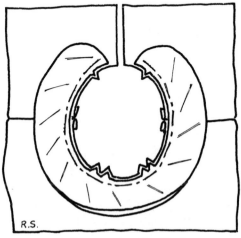

Collar on right side of bodice

4. Fold back the front extensions on the fold line so that the balance
    points match.
    Cut a cross-way strip 2.5cm wide in matching material (a lighter
    weight material may be used on woollen fabrics).
    Pin the cross-way strip on top of the collar and overlapping front
    extension. The turning allowance line on strip should lie on top of
    the seam line at neck edge. Pin, tack and stitch through the seam
    line from the fold line of one front extension to the fold line of the
    other front extension.
    Trim turning allowances to 6mm and snip the curved parts.

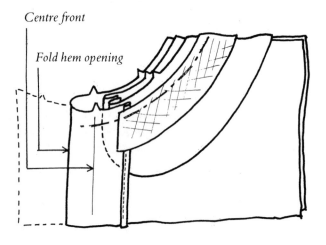

Matching the balance points

5. Lift the collar up from the bodice and fold the front extension and
    cross-way strip to the wrong side. Pull row of machining into
    position and pin and tack.
    Turn under the free edge of the cross-way strip and pin and tack in
    position to the bodice as for a cross-way facing.
    Hem into position.

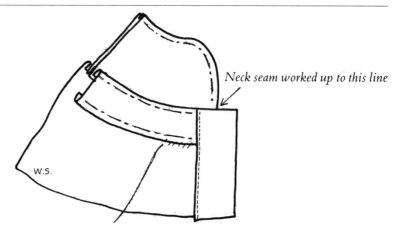

Neck seam worked up to this line

W.S.

Collar lifted up from bodice

Stand Up Styles

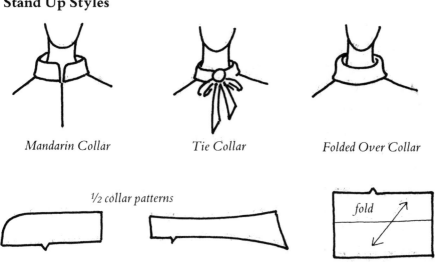

Mandarin Collar *Tie Collar* *Folded Over Collar*

½ collar patterns

fold

Three styles

The method for these three collars is very similar.

1. Mandarin Collar. Only baste interfacing to the wrong side of the collar.
2. At neck edge of the collar facing, turn the seam allowance to wrong side and tack. For tie collar, snip through turning at centre front mark.

Dealing with collar facing

3.   With right side facing, pin, tack and machine the two collar sections together on the seam line.
     Remove tacks.
     Layer the turning to a maximum width of 6mm and snip the curved parts.
     Turn the collar (and ties) to the right side, work seam to the edge and pin and tack into position.

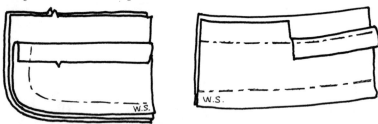

Making the collar

4.   Seams and darts into the neck edge should be complete.

Prepare front opening

(a) Fold back the front extensions or apply the front facings and stitch as far as centre front line.
     Snip through the seam allowance at this point and trim off the shaded parts.

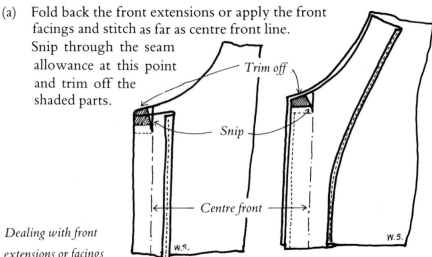

Dealing with front

extensions or facings

Turn the front extensions or the facing to the wrong side.
Baste flat to the bodice.

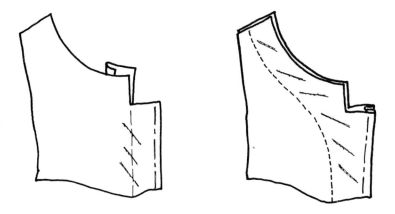

Turn extensions or facings in and baste

(b)   Opening may also be a faced slit or a zip opening which should be
      completed in the usual way. In this case, the collar will fit right to
      the edge of the opening.

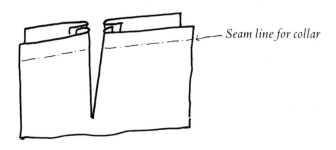

Seam line for collar

Faced slit opening

5.   Place the collar on right side of the bodice, matching centre back
     and centre fronts of the collar and the bodice.
6.   Pin, tack and machine collar to the bodice along the seam line.
     Trim turnings to 6mm. Snip the curved parts. Remove tacks.

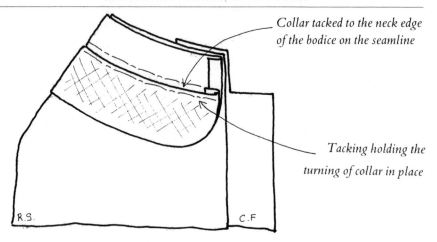

Collar tacked to the neck edge of the bodice on the seamline

Tacking holding the turning of collar in place

Attaching the collar

7.   Lift collar up and press the turnings into the collar.
      Bring the tacked edge of the collar facing to the line of machining.
      Pin and tack into position.
      Hem through the machine stitches so that no stitches are visible on
      the right side.

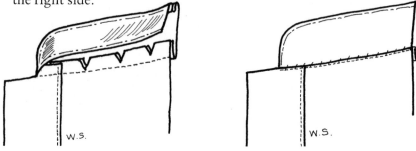

Collar turnings trimmed and hemmed inside

Straight turn-over Collar – worn open or closed.

Turn-over Collar   *½ collar pattern*

A.   One method of making and setting on this collar is very similar to the method for the mandarin collar **BUT** when the collar is set to the neck edge it is placed to the **WRONG** side of the bodice.

This seam is layered and snipped in the same way and then turned to the RIGHT side of the bodice. The hemming stitches will be hidden when the collar is folded over to its final position whether it is worn closed or open.

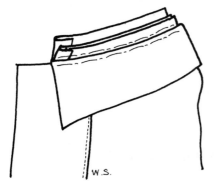

*Collar tacked to neck edge
of bodice on seam line*

Tacked neck edge of under collar

W.S.

Attaching a turn-over collar

B.   An alternative method of setting on this collar is to put the collar between the bodice and the shaped facing.

1.   The interfacing is basted to the wrong side of the upper collar.

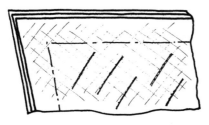

Interfacing basted to W.S. of upper collar

2. With right sides facing, the under collar is pinned, tacked and machined to the upper collar along the seam line. Remove tacks and layer the seam turnings. Snip any curves and clip off the sharp corners.

3. Turn the collar to the right side, working the seam to the edge – use a pin to ease out sharp corners. Tack around the edge and baste through the middle of the collar.

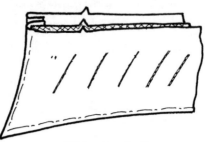

Right side of collar

4. Place the collar to the right side of the bodice matching centre back and centre front. Pin, tack very securely through the seam line.

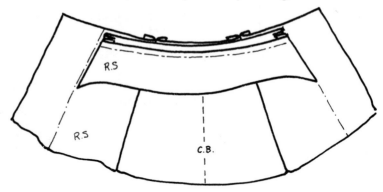

Collar in place

5. Join seams in the facing, neaten the unnotched edge and lay over the collar with right sides facing, matching seams and balance points. Pin, tack and machine along the seam line.
    Remove tacks.
    Layer the seam turnings and snip curves and clip corners.
    The facing is now turned to the wrong side. Lift the collar up and tack through all thicknesses just below the seam.

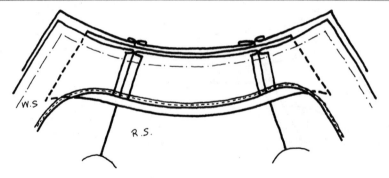

Collar hidden between bodice and facing

6. Hem the facing to seam turnings at both shoulders.

Facing hemmed to shoulder Seam turnings

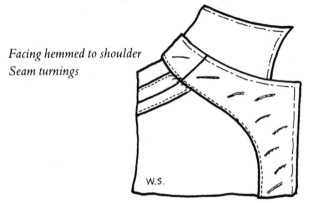

Inside of collar showing facing

C. Another alternative is to use a crossway facing instead of a shaped facing at the back neck. This would be turned under between the shoulder seams and hemmed to the bodice.

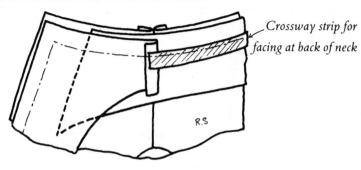

Crossway strip for facing at back of neck

Placing crossway strip

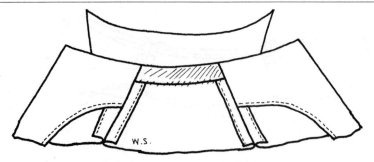

Crossway strip neatened at back neck

Traditional Shirt Collar

This collar sits very well if a tie or scarf is to be worn. The collar is really in two parts – the fall, which is the part which is visible when the garment is on, and the stand which fits snugly round the neck.

Shirt collar

½ collar pattern

The fall is made in exactly the same way as the straight collar – i.e. with right sides facing, pin, tack and machine the upper interfaced collar to the under collar. Remove tacks. Layer the seam turnings, clip corners and snip curves. Turn to the right side, work seam to the edge and tack around stitched edge.

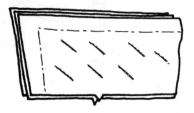

Interfacing basted to collar

The Stand or neckband. Baste the interfacing to the wrong side of the stand, or neckband.

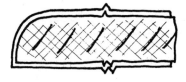

The Stand

2.   Tack in the seam allowance on the neck edge of stand facing.

Stand facing

3.   Place the right side of the stand and fall together and pin and tack along the seam line.

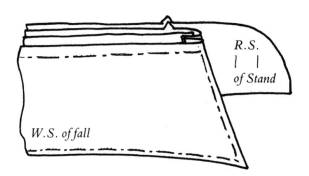

Stand and fall with right sides together

4.   Pin stand facing with wrong side uppermost, over the collar.
Tack and machine on the seam line.
Layer the seam allowance and snip curves.

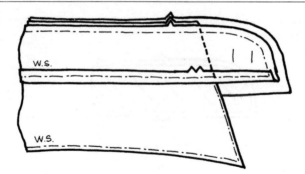

Stand facing placed over collar

5.   Turn the stand of collar right sides out. Press.

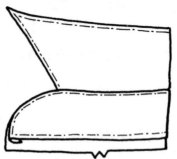

Collar and stand right sides out

6.   Matching balance points and seam lines, pin the right side of the stand to the right side of the neck edge. Tack and machine. Layer the seam turnings. Snip curves.

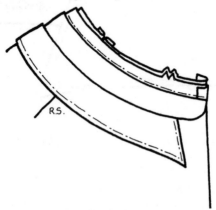

Stand tacked to neck edge

7. Fold the free edge of stand to the wrong side and pin close to the row of machining. Tack. Hem through machining so that no stitches are visible on the right side.

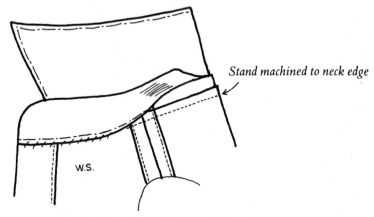

Stand machined to neck edge

W.S.

Stand machined and facing hemmed

Roll Collar

1. Sometimes the under collar is cut separately and has to be joined to front and back bodice sections first.

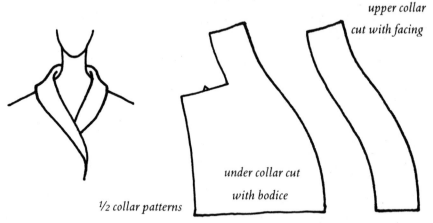

upper collar
cut with facing

under collar cut
with bodice

½ collar patterns

Roll collar and pattern pieces

2. Stay-stitch the front neck corner and snip diagonally through the turning at this point.

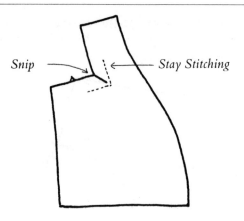

Prepare under collar

3. With right sides facing, pin front and back bodice at shoulders, matching balance points and seam lines. Tack, machine and neaten. At neck edge, the stitching must not go beyond exact corner of the seam line.

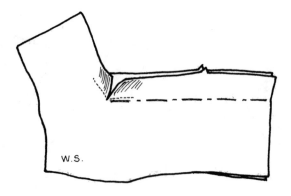

Machine shoulder seams

4. Join back seams of the collar extensions on front sections. Press open.
    Join neck edge of collar extensions to back neck of bodice.
    At shoulders this stitching must exactly meet the stitching of the shoulder seam.

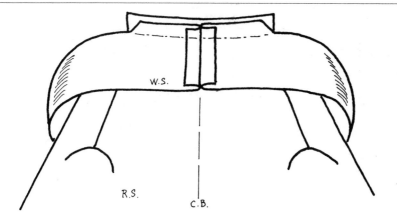

Join back of collar extensions

5. Baste interfacing to wrong side of the upper collar and front facing. Join centre back seams.

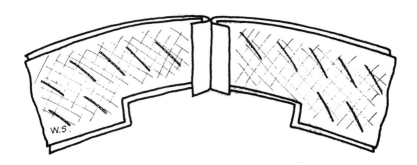

Interfacing basted in place

6. Place right side of facing to right side of bodice matching balance points and seam lines.
   Pin, tack and machine on the seam line.
   Remove tacks.
   Layer seam turnings and clip the curves.
   Snip inner corners of neck edge of facing.

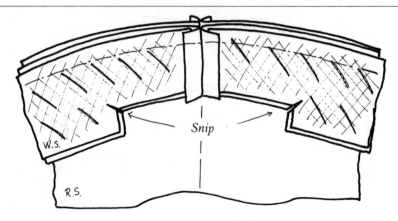

Facing attached to bodice

7. Turn the facing to the wrong side, work seam to the edge and tack into position.
    Baste through the centre facing.
    At neck, trim seam allowance to 1cm and snip. Turn under and tack so that the seam line of the facing lies on the machining. Hem through the machining so that no stitches show on the right side. Hem the facing extension to seam turning at the shoulder. Press. Roll collar to right side.

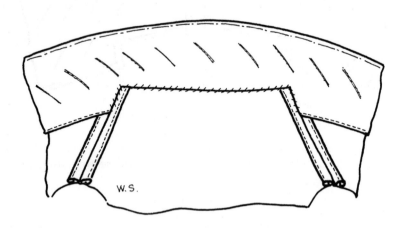

Facings turned in and neatened

16

CUFFS

Cuffs can take a variety of forms to finish the lower edge of a sleeve, whether long or short.

1. The simplest form of a cuff is really an extension of the sleeve folded back.

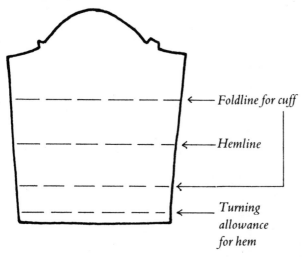

← Foldline for cuff

← Hemline

← Turning allowance for hem

Pattern of sleeve with hem and cuff lines marked in

2. The sleeve seam is stitched and neatened according to the type of fabric.

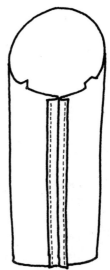

Seamed sleeve

3. The hem is turned to the wrong side on the hem line and tacked
    into position. The free edge of the hem is turned under, tacked into
    position and slip hemmed.

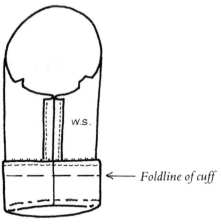

<- — Foldline of cuff

Hemmed Sleeve

4. The hem is turned to the right side along the fold line for the cuff
    and tacked into position.
    Press lightly. Remove tackings and press again.

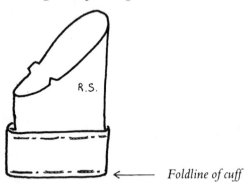

<- — Foldline of cuff

Cuff turned up on right side of sleeve

Turnback cuff for short sleeve

1. This may be either a straight band or a shaped cuff rather like a
    collar.
    The cuff is interfaced, and pinned, tacked and machined on seam
    line. The turnings are layered and snipped at corners and curves.

Two cuff shapes

2. Turn the cuff to the right side and tack round the edge.
   Baste through the middle of the cuff.

Right side of cuffs

3. Place the prepared cuff to the right side of the sleeve matching the
   balance points and seam lines. Pin and tack through the seam line.

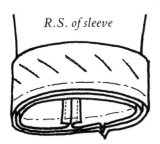 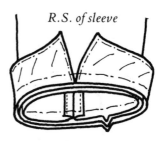

Cuffs placed on sleeves

4. Pin and tack a crossway strip 2.5cm wide on top of the cuff.
   This may be in self material if thin or in toning material if the
   garment is in thick material.
   Make the final join in the crossway strip so that it fits snugly on the
   cuff.
   Machine into position on the seam line. Remove tacking stitches.
   Trim and layer turnings.

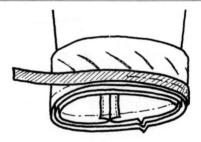

Placing Crossway strip

5. Pull the cuff down from the sleeve and press the turnings onto the sleeve. Turn under the free edge of the crossway strip and pin and tack to the sleeve. Either hem or machine into position. Remove tacks and press.

Crossway strip stitched in place

6. The cuff is now folded back to the right side of the sleeve and pressed into position.

Finished cuffs

Full sleeve set into a cuff which fastens

1. **Preparation of sleeve**

> The sleeve seam must be stitched and neatened.
> The sleeve opening must be completed.
> The fullness in the sleeve must be arranged.

2. **Preparation of cuff**. Baste the interfacing to the wrong side of the cuff.

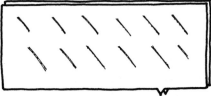

Basted interfacing

3. On the cuff facing, turn the seam allowance at sleeve edge to the wrong side and tack into position.

Cuff facing

4. Place the right sides of cuff and cuff facing together so that the seam lines match. Pin, tack and machine on the seam line on 3 edges of cuff (leave sleeve edge open). Trim and layer turning allowances. Snip curves and corners. Remove tacking stitches.

Seams on 3 edges of cuff

5. Turn the cuff to the right side and work the seam to the edge. Tack round the 3 machined edges of cuff. Baste through the middle of the cuff.

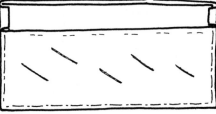

Right side of cuff

6. Place the right side of cuff to the right side of the sleeve matching balance points and seam lines. Check that both sides of the cuff opening are the same length. Check that fullness is arranged correctly.

Pin, tack and machine through the seam line.

Remove tacking stitches and gathering threads.

Trim turning allowance to 0.5cms.

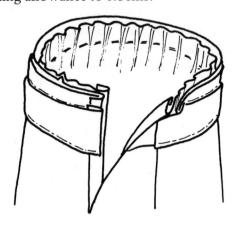

Sew right sides together

7. The cuff is pulled down from the sleeve and the turnings are pressed to the inside of the cuff. The fold of the cuff facing is placed over the turnings just to the line of machining. Pin, tack and hem into position. The cuff may be top stitched if required. Complete the cuff with fastening e.g. button and buttonhole. There are many variations to the shape of the cuff but the method is basically the same.

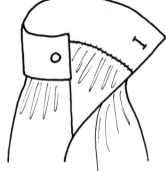

Finished cuff and sleeve opening

17

POCKETS

Apart from being very useful, pockets can be an important fashion feature on a garment, or they can be concealed in a seam. They should be large enough to take the hand of the wearer comfortably.

Patch Pocket

1. Fold under a 0.5cm turning to the wrong side at the top edge of the pocket. Tack and stitch.

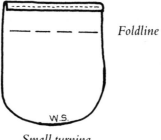

Foldline

Small turning

2. Fold the hem facing to the right side along the fold line. Pin and tack into position along the seam lines at the sides of the pocket for the depth of the hem facing only. Machine. Trim turnings at sides to 0.5cm.

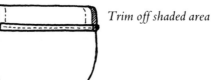

Trim off shaded area

Top Hem
167

3.   Fold the hem facing to the wrong side and tack along to top edge. Slip hem lower edge of hem facing. Snip the seam allowances on the curved edges of the pocket. Turn the seam allowances to the wrong side along the seam line and tack into position. Press lightly.

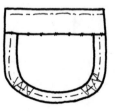

Pocket ready to put onto garment

4.   Position the pocket on the right side of the garment and pin and tack into place.
       The pocket is then stitched on, (usually by machining) with reinforcing at the corners.

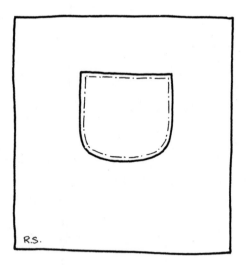

R.S.

Pocket positioned and tacked

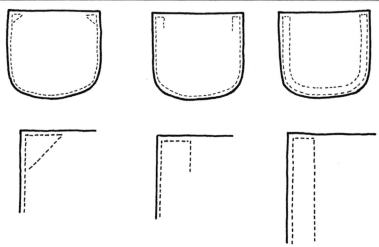

Various methods of stitching pocket and reinforcing corners

Alternative method of preparing the pocket

The pocket is cut double.

Fold along fold line with the right sides facing.

Pin, tack and stitch along the seam line leaving 2 to 3cm open at lower edge of pocket. Trim and snip seam allowances.

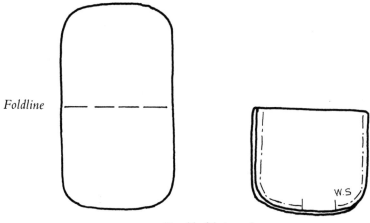

Foldline

W.S

Double fabric pocket

Turn the pocket to the right side and tack round the edge.

Tuck in the turnings at the gap in the stitching and tack together.

These will be sewn together as the pocket is machined to the garment.

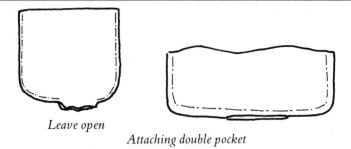

Leave open

Attaching double pocket

Bound Pocket

This is rather like a large bound buttonhole with layers of material sewn behind it which are stitched together to make the pocket.

1. The exact position of the pocket is marked on the right side of the garment.
   (This is usually done when the garment is thread marked).
2. The pocket strip is cut. This is most easily done if cut on one piece, but once the making of the pocket is understood, it is possible, and equally correct, to cut the strip in sections. The strip must be as wide as the opening + 4cms and long enough to bind the pocket, the pocket back and the pocket front. This strip can be cut in 1 or 3 sections. e.g. a pocket 12cm wide and 15cm deep would require a strip 14cm wide and 35cm deep, or 5,15 and 15cm. Tack a line on the right side of the strip 1cm below the middle of the strip and the exact width of the pocket opening.

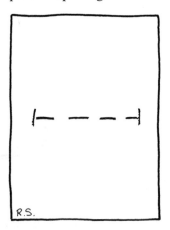

Tack pocket opening

3. Place the right side of the strip to the right side of the garment so that the two tacking lines are together.
    Pin and tack through the pocket line.
    Tack two lines the length of the pocket opening 0.5cm away from the pocket line.
    Machine round the pocket line in a very accurate rectangle 1.0cm wide by the length of the pocket opening.

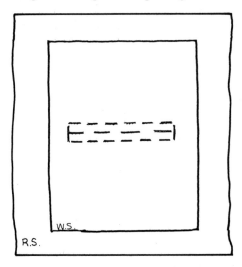

Sew round pocket opening

4. Cut the centre line of pocket and diagonally to the four corners.

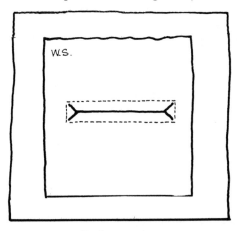

Pocket opening cut

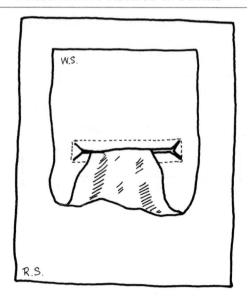

5.   Take both ends of the pocket strip through the pocket opening to the wrong side of the garment and use it to form a binding round the cut edges.

      Diagonally baste the inverted pleat in the centre of the pocket.

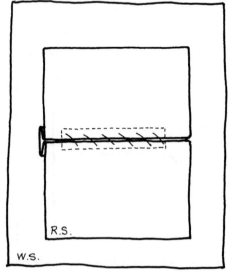

Baste inverted pleat

6. On the right side, machine round the pocket opening through all the layers of material. (Be sure that the pocket strip is flat on the wrong side of the garment.)

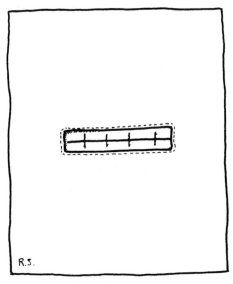

R.S.

Machined pocket opening

7. On the wrong side fold the pocket back down over the pocket front.

Fold back on this line of stitching

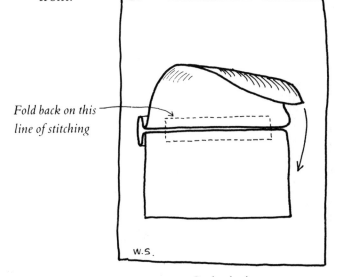

W.S.

Pocket back

W.S.

Folded down

8. Pin, tack and machine the pocket sections together rounding off
    the lower corners of the pocket and lifting the pocket away from
    the garment as this stitching does not show on the right side.
    Trim the turning allowances to 1.0cm and neaten with overcasting
    or zigzagging.

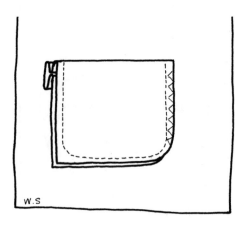

W.S

Stitch pocket and neaten

Welt Pocket

This is very similar in the making to a bound pocket but the appearance on the right side is of one straight band or welt.

1. The pocket welt is cut the length of the pocket opening plus 2 turnings and twice the required depth plus 2 turnings.
2. Baste interfacing to one half of welt and catch stitch along the fold line. Fold the welt in half with the right sides facing and stitch the two ends on the seam line. Turn the welt to the right side. Tack round the edges and baste through the middle. Press lightly.

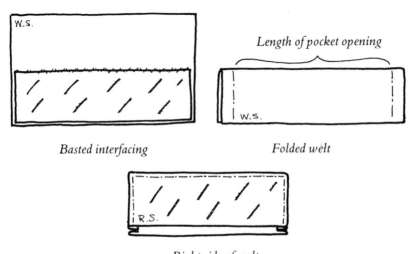

Basted interfacing   *Folded welt*

Right side of welt

3. Cut the pocket strip as for the bound pocket. Mark the pocket position on the garment (right side) and place the raw edges of the welt to this line.

    Pin and tack into position.

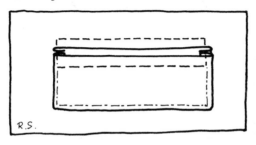

Welt tacked in position

4. Place and stitch the pocket strip as for the bound pocket.
    Cut as for the bound pocket.
    Push the pocket strip through to the wrong side of the garment but leave the welt on the right side. Bring both ends of the strip together to form the pocket.
    Stitch and neaten the pocket section as for the bound pocket.
    Overcast the top edge of the opening.

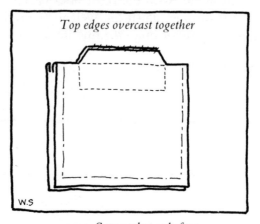

Sew pocket as before

5. On the right side lift the welt up to the final position and either invisably hem the sides of the welt to the garment or for extra strength, set the machine to satin stitch (buttonhole stitch on machine) and work over the end of the welt.

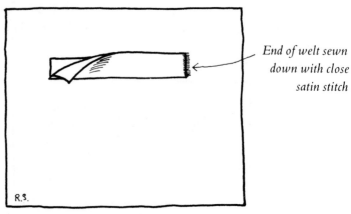

End of welt sewn down with close satin stitch

Finishing the welt

Pocket in Seam

This is a convenient pocket to use when pockets are not required as a style feature as it is made in with the seam.

1. The seam is usually designed with pocket extensions where the pocket is situated.

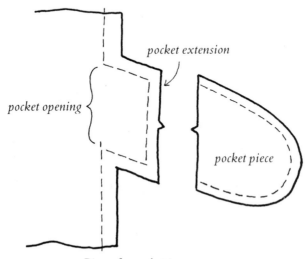

Pieces for pocket in seam

2. The pocket piece is joined to the pocket extension on both front and back sections of garment. The seam is neatened and pressed open.

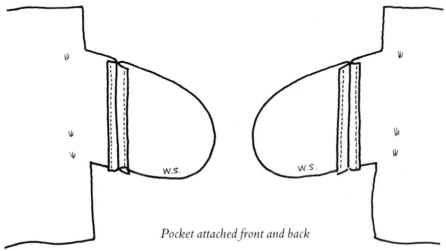

Pocket attached front and back

3. The two edges of the seam are now matched with the right sides facing.
    Pin, tack and stitch on the seam line leaving the pocket opening unstitched.
    Now stitch the pocket sections together.
    The seam edges are neatened separately by a method suitable for fabric of garment.
    The edges of the pocket are trimmed to 1.0cm and either overcast or zigzagged.

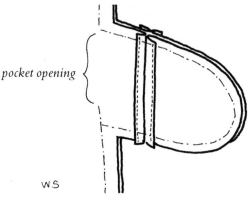

Front and back seams matched

4. Clip the back seam turning above and below the pocket extension. Press the seam open and press the pocket to the front along the fold line of the pocket opening.

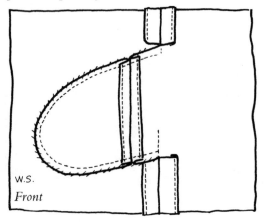

Press pocket to the front

Front Hip Pocket

This pocket has the pocket back and yoke section cut in one piece.

Hip pocket

Three pattern pieces go to make up this type of pocket.

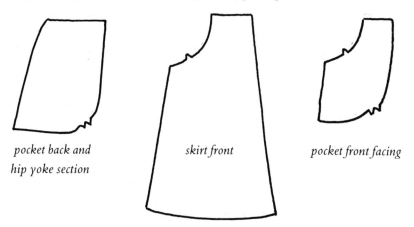

*pocket back and
hip yoke section*

skirt front

pocket front facing

Three pieces of front hip pocket

1. With the right sides together the pocket facing is pinned, tacked and machined to the skirt front along the pocket seam line.
    Trim and snip curved turnings.
    Turn the facing to the wrong side and tack along the seam.
    Press.

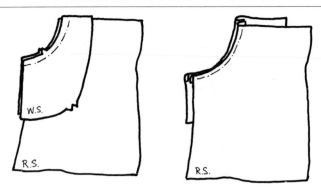

Stitch facing and turn in

2. Pin, tack and machine the hip yoke and pocket back to the pocket facing along the curved edge.

Trim the turnings to 1.0cm and neaten by overcasting and zigzagging.

Baste the pocket to the skirt at the side seam and the waist.

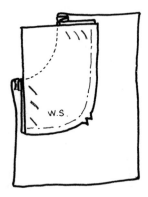

Hip yoke and pocket back in position

18

SLEEVES

Types or Styles of Sleeve

1. Smooth headed
    – basic sleeve

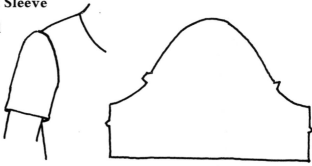

Smooth headed sleeve and pattern

2. Fitted sleeve – fits the arm snugly.

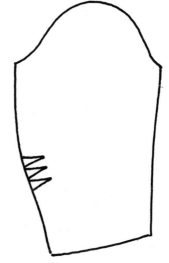

Fitted sleeve and pattern

3.   Puff sleeve – gathered at head and upper arm.

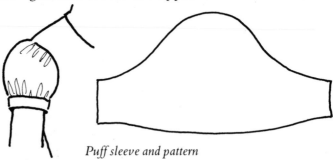

Puff sleeve and pattern

4.   Very full gathered sleeve – Bishops.

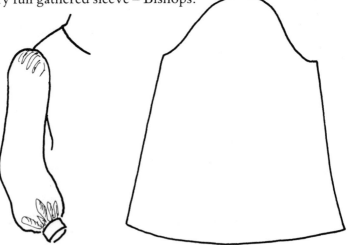

Bishops sleeve and pattern

5.   Cap sleeve. A very short sleeve often cut in one with the bodice.

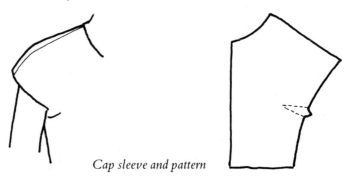

Cap sleeve and pattern

6. Magyar Sleeve. Cut in one with the bodice – both shoulder and underarm seam extended.

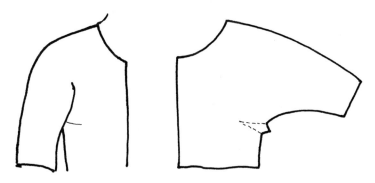

Magyar sleeve and pattern

7. Raglan sleeve. The sleeve seams run from the underarm to the neck line. The sleeve is either cut in 2 pieces or in one with a dart at the shoulder.

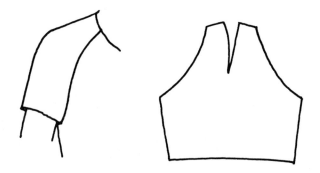

Raglan sleeve and pattern

A sleeve which is well set in should have the straight grain threads hanging vertically and no signs of stress at underarm.

For a smooth headed sleeve, there should be no pleats or gathers in the sleeve head.

For gathered sleeves, the gathers should be evenly distributed over the sleeve head.

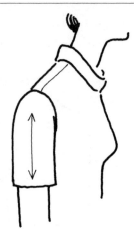

Sleeve hanging straight without stress

To make a pair of Sleeves

The head of the sleeve is hollowed out more at the front than the back to accommodate the shape of the front and back armhole and also to allow the arm to move forward. It is therefore essential to make a pair of sleeves and to set them into the correct armholes.

Where the material appears the same on both sides, fold the sleeves thus:

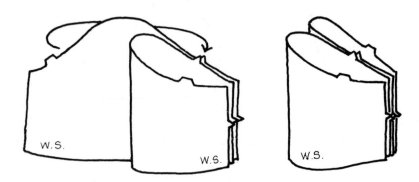

Folding a pair of sleeves

The position of the balance points can also be used to check that a pair of sleeves are made.

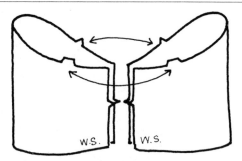

Pairing sleeves by balance points

To set in a Sleeve

Sleeves are cut with a certain amount of fullness to allow for the muscle at the top of the arm. This means that the sleeve head or top of the sleeve measures more than the armhole. For a sleeve which is smooth headed this amount will be 3 - 4cms. but very much more for a gathered sleeve.

1. Put in 2 rows of machine or hand gathering between the balance points – one on the seam line and one 0.3cm away in the seam allowance.

The seam or seams in a sleeve are made and neatened in the usual way.

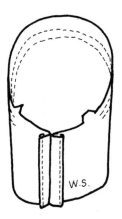

Gathering between balance points

2. With the right sides together match the sleeve seam to the underarm of seam of bodice. Pin seam on seam line as far as front and back balance points.

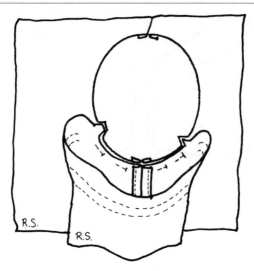

Sleeve and bodice seams aligned

3. From the inside of the garment place the top of sleeve head to the shoulder seam of the bodice. Pin. Pull up the threads to ease or gather the sleeve head and spread evenly over sleeve head.
    N.B. For a smooth headed sleeve this fullness should appear minimal. Pin, tack and machine on the seam line.

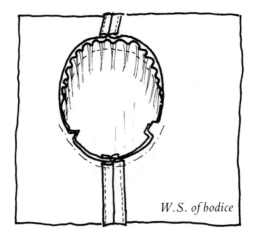

Sleeve set into armhole

4. For extra strength at the underarm seam, work a second row of machining very close to the first for the distance between the

balance points.

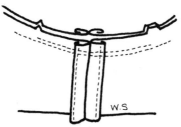

Double stitch underarm seam

To neaten armhole seam

Another row of machining is worked 1cm from the seam line, the turnings trimmed close to this and then overcast or zigzagged. The armhole turnings are pressed towards the sleeve.

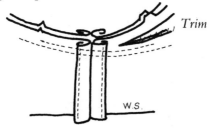

Neatening armhole seam

Shirt Sleeves

Shirt sleeves are usually set in by the flat method as the head of the sleeve is not so shaped as in a smooth headed or plain top sleeve. This method is also useful for other loose tops with a dropped shoulder line.

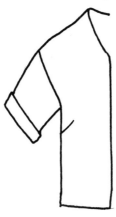

Dropped shoulder line

1.   The shoulder and yoke seams should be completed and neatened.

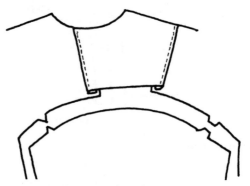

Setting in shirt sleeve

2.   With the wrong sides together the sleeve and armhole seam lines are matched. Pin, tack and machine along seam line.
Trim turning on the sleeve to 0.5cm and the turning on the armhole of bodice to 1.0cm.

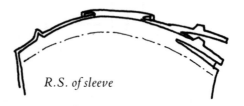

Trim turnings separately

3.   Fold the bodice turning over the sleeve turning and tack into position.

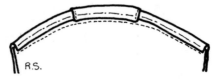

Tack turnings in position

4.   Open out sleeve and bodice sections and tack the seam flat to the sleeve as for a double stitched seam.
Machine.

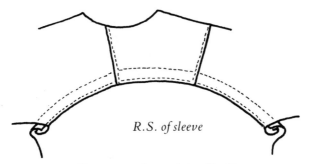

R.S. of sleeve

Flat seam at dropped shoulder line

5. The sleeve and underarm seam are then completed as one seam.

Raglan Sleeve

1. With the right sides together pin, tack and machine the sleeve front to the bodice front and the sleeve back to the bodice back.
   Balance points and seam lines should match as for all seams.

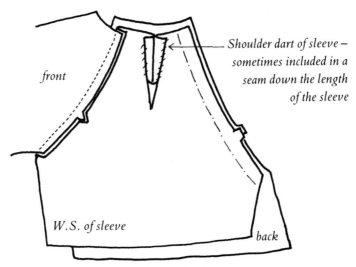

front

Shoulder dart of sleeve – sometimes included in a seam down the length of the sleeve

W.S. of sleeve

back

Raglan sleeve with shoulder dart

2. The seams are neatened by working a second row of maching 1cm away from the first and in the seam allowance.
   The turnings are trimmed close to the second row of machining and then overcast, blanket stitched or zigzagged.

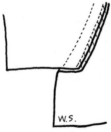

Neatening the seam

The turnings are pressed towards the sleeve. If the underarm end of the seam is very curved it may be snipped to make it lie flat. The under-arm and sleeve are then completed as one seam, making sure that the armhole seams lie exactly on top of one another.

Underarm Gusset for Magyar Type Sleeve

1. Reinforce the point of the gusset position by a line of machining. Slash to this point.

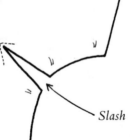

Slash

Slash reinforced

2. With the right sides facing join the gusset to the underarm slashed edges. The seam turning will be 1cm on the gusset but on the slashed edge will graduate from 1cm at the underarm to almost nothing at the pointed end of the slash.
    Neaten the seam by overcasting or zigzagging.

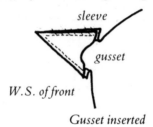

sleeve

gusset

W.S. of front

Gusset inserted

3. A second gusset is inserted in the same way to the underarm on the
    back of the garment.

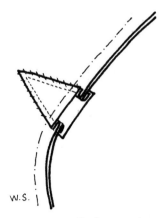

Back gusset inserted

The underarm seam is pinned, tacked and stitched on seam line.
Neaten the seam according to the type of fabric.

19

WAIST FINISHES

Trousers, culottes, skirts etc. need to be fitted to grip the waist comfortably. If the garment is too tight at the waist, horizontal puckers appear round the waist line and the garment tends to ride up, if the waist is too loose, the seam drops below the waistline and spoils the fit of the garment.

On childrens clothes and underwear the waist edge is sometimes elasticated.

1. The hem is turned in the normal way and tacked into position.
    It is usual for this waist finish to be machined at the top edge of the hem as well as at the lower edge. An opening is left in the lower edge through which the elastic is inserted.
    The elastic is joined with a flat seam and the hem machining is completed when the elastic is pushed back in the hem.
    The elastic should be just wide enough to fit between the two lines of machining – if it is wider or narrower it will curl and twist in the hem or casing.

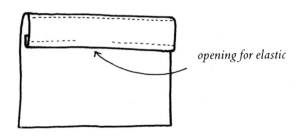

opening for elastic

Hem opening for elastic

2. Alternatively if the top edge of the garment is shaped, a crossway facing is used to form the casing for the elastic.

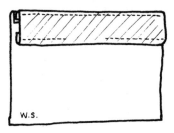

Casing for elastic

On adult garments the waist edge is usually set into a band. This may be a band of the same material or a band of petersham.

Band of the same Material

This is usually stiffened with interfacing for a professional finish, but on an apron it is permissable to leave the waistband unstiffened.

1. The band should be cut long enough to allow the pointed end to overlap the underwrap by approximately 5.0cms. An apron waistband is usually a straight ended band.
   If using a commercial pattern check the size of the band against the waist edge if there have been any alterations to waist size. Correct if necessary.

2. The interfacing is basted to the wrong side of the front of the waistband only. If the band has a fold at the top edge, the interfacing is catch-stitched to the fold line to prevent it moving out of place during wear. On the back of the band, snip the seam allowance at the points marking the extent of the overwrap and underwrap. Fold the seam allowance to the wrong side of back of the band and tack into position.

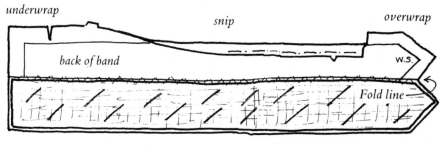

Waistband overlap for fastening the opening

3. Fold the waistband with the right sides together and seam lines matching. Pin, tack and machine the overwrap (pointed end) and the underwrap. Layer and trim the turnings at the two ends. Clip the corners. Snip the seam allowance on the front of band at the ends of underwrap and overwrap.

Waistband folded and stitched

4. Turn the waistband to the right side. Tack round the two ends and top edge.

Waistband turned in to right side

5. With the right sides facing and matching balance points and seam lines, place the waistband to the waist edge of the garment. Pin, tack and machine along the seam line.

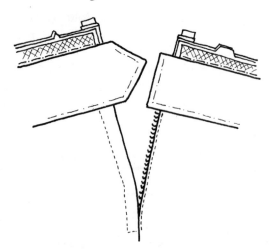

Waistband tacked to waist edge

6. Trim and layer the seam turnings. Remove the tacking stitches.
7. Lift the waistband up and tuck the waist edge turnings inside the band. Place the folded edge of the back of the band to the line of stitching. Pin and tack into position. Hem through the machine stitches. Remove all the tacking stitches and press.

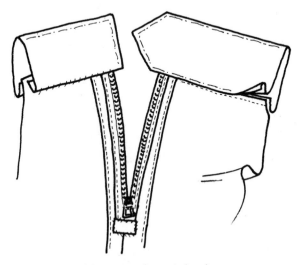

Neatening the waistband

Petersham

With this waist finish there is no band visible on the right side as the petersham fits on inside the waistline.
1. Cut the petersham the length of waist plus turnings of 3cm.
2. Turn a double hem (0.5cm and then 1cm) onto the wrong side of the petersham at each end of the band.
   Hem into position very securely.

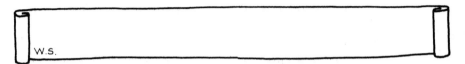

W.S.

Petersham with hemmed ends

3. Place the right side of the petersham to the wrong side of the waist edge of the skirt. The edge of the petersham should just touch the

seam line at the waist. The ends of the petersham should be level with the finished opening of the skirt.
Pin, tack and machine close to the edge of the petersham.

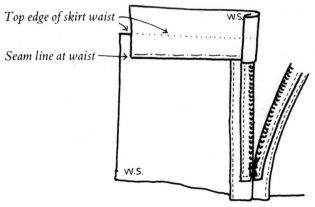

Petersham placed at waist

4.   The waist turning is then trimmed off to 0.5cm. from the machine stitching.

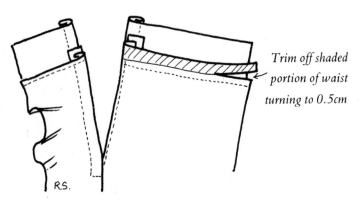

Trim off shaded portion of waist turning to 0.5cm

Trimming the waist seam

5.   Cover the raw edge of the waist turning with seam binding. Pin and tack seam binding into position. If the petersham is unboned this may then be machined, but if the petersham is boned, it should be sewn into position by hand using hemming stitches.

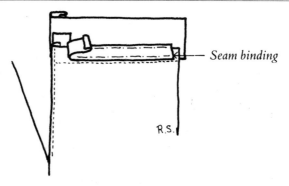

Neatening the waist

6. Fold the petersham to the wrong side and press.
7. Sew on hooks and eyes so that ends of petersham just meet.

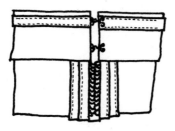

Waist fastenings on petersham

Shaped Facings

The waist edge may be finished by a shaped facing. It is essential that a firm interfacing be used so that the waist edge does not stretch.

20

FASTENINGS

Garment fastenings should last the life of the garment and therefore their choice will be influenced by –
1)   The type of garment
2)   The material of the garment
3)   The position of the fasteners on the garment
4)   The age of the wearer
5)   The method required for cleaning the garment
6)   Whether the fastening is also required to be decorative

Wherever possible fastenings should be sewn onto double fabric.

Tapes and Ribbons

1.   Measure the width of the tape and fold over this amount onto wrong side of tape.

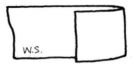

Turning on tape

2.   Place wrong side of tape to inside of garment so that the turned end of tape is just below the edge of the garment.
Pin and tack into position.

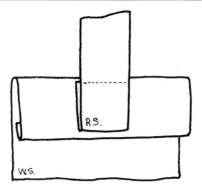

Attach to inside of garment

3. Hem three sides of tape and leave thread attached.

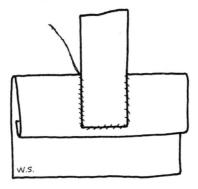

Tape end hemmed on 3 sides

4. From right side of garment, fold tape level with edge of **garment** and oversew edge of garment to tape.

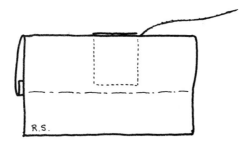

Oversew fourth side with tape folded back

Where the edges of opening meet, the second tape will be sewn on in exactly the same way on the opposite side of the opening.

Where the edges of the opening overlap

1. The position of the overwrap should be marked by a line of tacking on the underwrap.

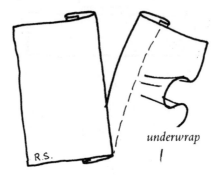

Opening with overlapping edges

2. The tape is positioned on right side so that the turned end is just short of line for overwrap.
    Pin and tack in position.
    The tape may then be machined or backstitched.
    On the overwrap position tape to edge of opening level with the other tape.

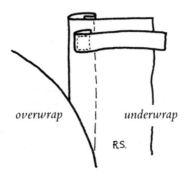

Positioning the tape

3. Free ends of tapes are finished with a very small hand sewn hem.

Tape end

4. Free ends of ribbon are cut diagonally to stop fraying.

Ribbon cut to stop fraying

Snap Fasteners (sometimes called press studs or poppers)

There are two parts to this type of fastener.

(a) a knobbed section on a flat base which goes on the wrong side of the overwrap.

(b) a thicker socket section which goes on the right side of the underwrap.

The overwrap section

1. Fasten the thread on with a small double stitch in the centre of the position for the fastener.

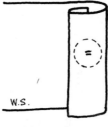

W.S.

Placing fastener

2. Anchor the fastener on with a single oversewing stitch in each hole.

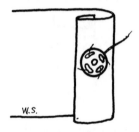

Anchoring the fastener

3. Buttonhole stitch or oversewing may be used to sew the fastener on, but the former is the stronger stitch. Whichever stitch is used, an uneven number of stitches should be worked in each hole and the same number in each hole. This should never be less than 5 stitches and will need to be more for larger fasteners. Fasten off thread with small double stitch close to the fastener.

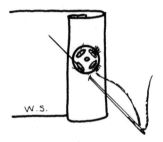

Sewing the fastener on

The Underwrap Section

Chalk the knob of the overwrap section and fold onto underwrap so that the opening is in the closed position. This will mark the centre position for the socket on the underwrap. This section is then sewn on in exactly the same way as the knobbed section.

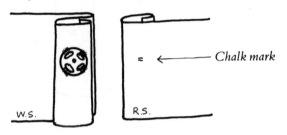

Placing second half of fastener

Hooks and Eyes or Bars

This is a very secure way of fastening outer clothing which is close fitting.

Hooks and Eyes are used on openings which do not have a wrap i.e. the opening meets edge to edge.

Hooks and Bars are used on openings which overwrap.

Hooks and Eyes or Bars come in various sizes from 00 (very small) upwards. The size should be chosen for the type of material and the amount of strain the fastening is likely to have put on it.

The Hook portion is sewn on first and goes on the wrong side of the overwrap.

1.   The hook is positioned with the edge of hook level with the edge of overwrap.

     The hook is held steady with a single oversewing stitch in each loop and one under the hook.

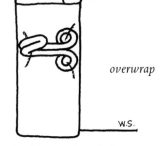

overwrap

W.S.

Placing the hook

2.   Buttonhole stitch is now worked round each loop so that they are each completely covered.

     The shaft is secured by at least 3 more stitches under the hook. Fasten off securely.

     N.B.   No stitches should show on the right side of the overwrap.

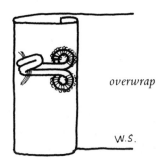

overwrap

W.S.

Stitching on the hook

The Eye should be sewn to the wrong side of the opposite edge of opening, so that the eye protrudes sufficiently for the hook to pass through it.

1. Hold the eye in the required position by a single oversewing stitch in each loop and either side of the eye at the edge of the opening.

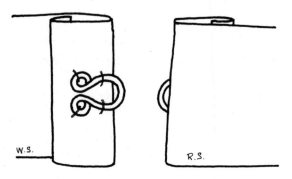

Positioning the eye

2. The loops of the eye are buttonhole stitched into position and the eye held down securely at the edge of the fastening with several oversewing stitches.

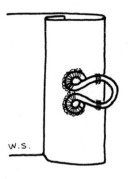

Stitching on the eye

Bars may be metal or worked in thread and are sewn to the right side of the underwrap.

1. The position of the bar is found by closing the opening and tacking in line to which this comes on the underwrap.

   The bar will be just inside this line and on a level with the hook.

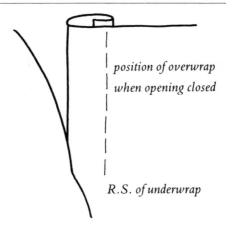

*position of overwrap
when opening closed*

R.S. of underwrap

Finding the position for the bar

2. The bar is held in position by a single oversewing stitch in each loop and then securely buttonhole stitched into position.
   Fasten off thread.

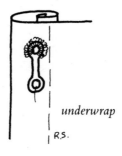

underwrap

R.S.

Stitching on the bar

Worked Bar

1. Position as for metal bar. The thread is fastened on with a double stitch.
   A straight stitch is taken across the material where a small portion of the material is taken up.

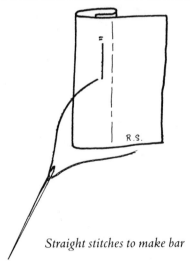

Straight stitches to make bar

2.   The thread is taken back to the other end of the stitch and the process repeated 4 or 5 times.
     Buttonhole stitch is then worked over resultant bar.
     Fasten off thread securely.

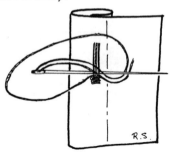

Working the bar

Trouser Hook and Bar

This is a much more substantial fastening for use on thicker materials and is particularly suitable for men's trousers.

Trouser hook and bar

To sew on Hook

1. The hook is sewn between the layers of the waistband and must be attached before the end of the waistband is sewn.

    The hook end of the fastening is attached with oversewing to the turned in seam allowance at end of waistband.

    A short length of tape is threaded through the other end of hook and hemmed to the interfacing.

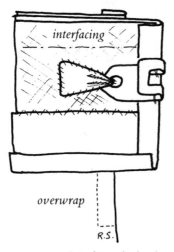

Attaching the hook

2. The waistband is folded over to wrong side and hemmed through the machining. On the waistband extension the waistband is tucked under the hook and the ends of the band invisibly sewn together by hand.

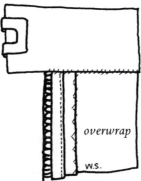

Finishing hook end of waistband

The Bar

3.   The bar is placed just inside the position of the overwrap when the opening is closed so that the bar will not be seen when the hook is fastened into it.

The bar is buttonhole stitched into position.

Fasten off thread securely.

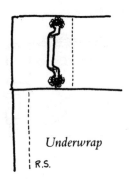

Placing and attaching the bar

Buttons

These come in a wide variety of shapes, colours and sizes, with or without a shank.

A shank is that portion of the button which holds the button slightly away from the fabric so that the layer of fabric from the other side of the garment can lie flat beneath the button when the two are fastened together.

Button without shank   *Button with shank*

Position of button

This is usually marked on commercial patterns.

Otherwise, close the opening in the correct position and mark the position of buttons on the underwrap by putting pins through the buttonholes where the centre line of garment crosses the buttonhole.

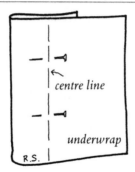

Marking the position of buttons

To sew on button

1. Use single thread of matching colour. On heavier materials use linen button thread of near shade. Fasten thread on with a double backstitch, hold the button in position and sew up and down through holes in the buttonhole – either hold the button slightly off material or work over a matchstick.

    Continue working in this way until the button is securely held, making sure that the stitches are in exactly the same place each time.

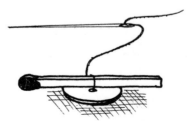

Allowing for a worked shank

2. Withdraw the matchstick and wind the thread round the threads between the button and the material.

    Take needle through to underside of work.

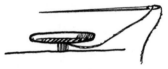

Working the shank

3. Now work buttonhole stitch over the 'bar' of stitches formed by stitching on the button.
    Fasten off securely.

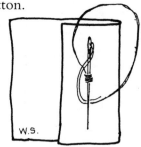

Finishing off

NOTE: If the button has a shank built into it there is no need to use a matchstick to work over – otherwise proceed in the same way.

Buttonholes

Position and size of buttonholes

These are usually marked on commercial patterns, but the following points should be noticed.

1) Buttonholes are horizontal when the strain is in this direction. Where the strain is sufficient to pull the button to one end of the buttonhole, a buttonhole with one round and one square end is used.

2) Buttonholes are vertical when the strain is in this direction or when the garment is loosely fitting and there is no strain. When there is no strain a buttonhole with two square ends is used.

Position of buttonholes on blouse front

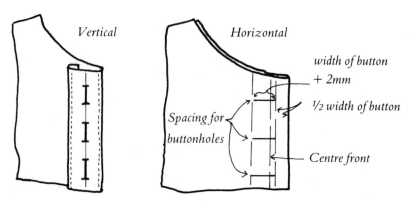

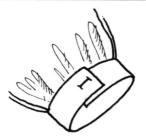

Position of buttonhole on cuff

Method of working buttonhole by hand – Worked Buttonhole

One round end and one square end. Use thread (single) of matching colour and weight. A buttonhole 2.5cm in length will use approximately 1 metre of thread.

1. Starting at the end of the buttonhole furthest from the folded edge, attach thread with double stitch and work rectangle of running stitch round the mark for buttonhole. The length of the rectangle is equal to the length of the button + 2mm and the width of the rectangle is 4mm.
    DO NOT CUT OFF THREAD.

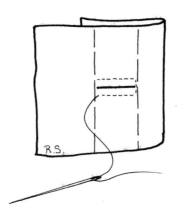

Work running stitch round buttonhole

2. Fold buttonhole marking in half and start the cut for the buttonhole on the folded edge.
    Open material flat again and complete the cut to each end of buttonhole.

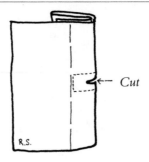

Cutting the buttonhole

3. Needle is put in slit and brought out just below line of running stitch in preparation to work buttonhole stitch along this edge.

   Take the double thread from the eye of the needle and place it under the point of the needle from left to right.

   Draw needle through fabric and pull away from worker so that the knot forms on the edge of the buttonhole.

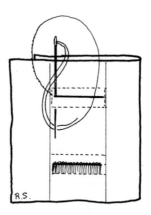

Buttonhole stitching

4. To work the round end, an uneven number of straight oversewing stitches is worked in a semi-circle at the end nearest to the fold (not less than 5 stitches).

   Bring out the needle at the end of the second side ready to work buttonhole stitch along this edge.

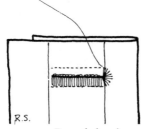

Rounded end

5. The second side of buttonhole complete.

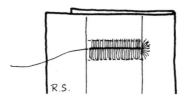

Two sides and one end

6. To work the square end, make 2 or 3 long stitches across the width of the buttonhole. Work buttonhole stitch over this bar with the knots on the inside of the buttonhole.
   Fasten off securely.

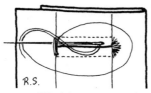

Working square end

Buttonhole with 2 square ends

1. Proceed as before but omit working the round end.
   Work one square end as before.

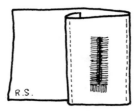

Omit rounded end

2. Now fasten the thread on at the other end of the buttonhole and work another bar.

Work second bar

Machine Made Buttonholes are a quick and serviceable substitute for hand worked buttonholes.

These may be made on any machine that does zigzag.

The stitch and tension should be set so that a close satin stitch is achieved.

Fix on the special buttonhole foot supplied with the machine.

The actual method varies slightly with the different makes of machine, but the main principles are the same. Consult the instruction booklet supplied with the machine for details.

1. Mark the position of the buttonhole as usual.

    With short stitch and narrow width work one side of buttonhole.

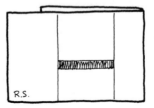

First side

2. With same stitch length but wide throw to stitch, work several long stitches across the end of buttonholes.

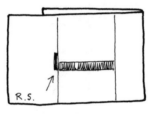

First bar

3.   With narrow stitch work second side of buttonhole.

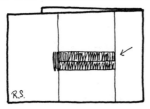

Second side

4.   With wide stitch work several long stitches at the end of but-
     tonhole.
     Fasten off all ends of thread.
     Pins are placed at each end of buttonhole to stop 'quick unrip'
     slipping whilst cutting the buttonhole.

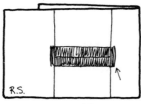

Second bar

Bound Buttonholes

These are not so strong as worked buttonholes and are not suitable for
frequently washed garments, or for use on transparent or bulky
materials.

1.   Mark the position as for hand worked buttonholes.

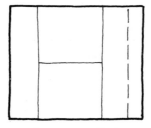

Position marked

2.   Cut the strip the length of the buttonhole + 3cms and 5cms wide.
     The selvedge threads should be along the length of the strip or the
     strips may be cut on the true cross for decorative purposes.
     Mark the centre of strip with tacking stitches.

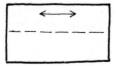

Centre marked strip

3. Place right side of strip to right side of garment and so that the centre of strip lies exactly on top of the buttonhole marking on the garment.
    Baste the strip into position.

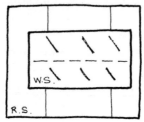

Positioning the strip

4. From the wrong side machine a very exact rectangle round the marking for the buttonhole. It should be the exact length of the buttonhole and 2mm on either side of centre mark for buttonhole. Fasten off securely.
    Cut centre line of buttonhole and cut to all four corners.

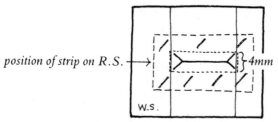

Machine rectangle and cut buttonhole

5. Push the strip through cut for buttonhole – to finish on wrong side.

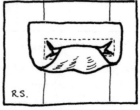

Push strip through

6. Pull the strip closely and evenly round the turnings so that a small inverted pleat is formed at each end of the strip.
Baste the edges of the bind together.
Press lightly.
Oversew the ends of the pleat together.

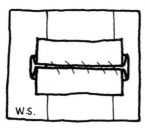

Neaten strip on wrong side

7. Attach the facing and turn to the wrong side.
Baste into position round each buttonhole.
Push pins through all the corners of the buttonhole.

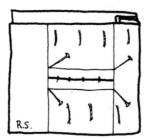

Baste facing in position

8. Cut the facing in the same manner as the buttonhole was originally cut – the corners are marked by the pins.

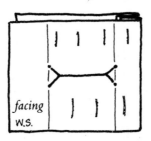

Cut buttonhole in facing

9. Turn under the cut edges of the facing and hem closely to the binding.

    Remove all tacking stitches and press.

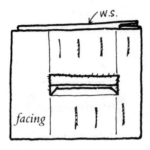

Neaten the facing

Buttonhole Loops

These are generally made at the edge of a garment. Use thread which matches the fabric of the garment.

1. Mark the centre of each buttonloop and also the diameter of the button.

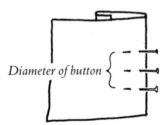

Pins at loop centre and button width

2. Attach thread at point A with a firm double stitch.

    Take needle to point B and pull the thread till rather less than a semi circle is left and work a double stitch at B.

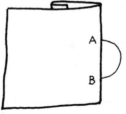

Starting the loop

3. Work several more strands from A to B according to the size of the loop.
    Work close buttonhole stitches over the strands taking the first and last stitches into the material.
    Fasten off securely.

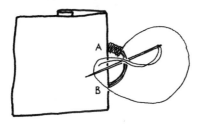

Buttonhole stitching the loop

Rouleau Loops

These form a decorative fastening, but are only suitable for fine and medium weight firm fabrics.

1. Cut crossway strips the length of the loop + 2.5cm. Where several loops are made, join sufficient crossway strips to make the rouleau all at once. The crossway strip should not be less than 2.5cms wide.
2. Fold the right side of the strip together and tack down the middle. The strip is machined the finished width of the rouleau from the fold of the strip. The finer the material the narrower the width of the rouleau. DO NOT CUT off the ends of machining.
    Trim the turnings on the strip to slightly less than the finished width of the rouleau.

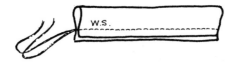

Wrong side of tube

3. Tie a blunt ended needle e.g bodkin to the ends of the machining and push down the tube.
    Carefully ease the two layers over one another until the tube is turned right side out.

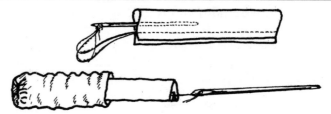

Turning tube right side out

4. Mark the positions of the loops on seam line and right side of garment.
    Mark the depth of the loops by a line of tacking *behind* the seam line.

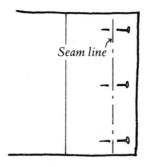

Seam line

Mark loop positions

5. Arrange the rouleau to form loops between the pins and between the two lines marking the depth of the loops.
    Pin firmly.
    Machine close to the seam line but in the seam allowance to anchor the loops firmly in position.

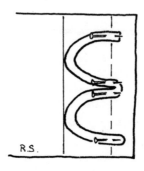

R.S.

Pin loops in position

6. Place the right side of the facing over the rouleau loops.
    Pin, tack and machine on the seam line.
    Trim turnings to 0.5cms and turn to the wrong side.

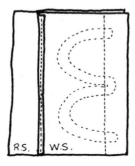

Facing placed over loops

7. The rouleau loops will now protrude from the edge of the garment.

Loops when facing is folded back

Velcro – Touch and Close Fastening is a modern fastening made from nylon. It consists of two strips which cling together because one side is composed of tiny hooks and the other of tiny loops. The strips are approximately 2cms wide and can be bought in a variety of colours.

cross section of Velcro

1. A square or strip of the looped side is sewn by hand to the underside of the overwrap. The stitches do not show on the right side.

2. A piece of the same size is sewn to the right side of the underwrap.
    N.B. The looped part of the Velcro strip is usually sewn to the wrong side of the overwrap and the hooked side to the right side of the underwrap.

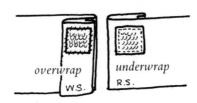

Velcro loops and hooks

Zips

There are several methods of inserting a zip.

Usually they are concealed in the opening, but occasionally they are used as a decorative feature when they have to be inserted into a slit.

Whatever method is used for a standard zip, it is always kept closed while it is being inserted – the reverse is true for an 'invisible' zip.

Zip into a slit

1. Stay stitch with machining round the lower end of the opening.

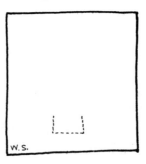

Stay stitching

2. Cut down the centre of the opening and diagonally to each corner. Fold back the turning allowance to the wrong side and tack into position.
    Press lightly.

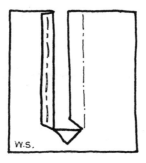

Cut the opening

3. The zip is placed centrally in the opening and pinned and tacked into position.
    The zip is then machined into position using a special one sided zip foot. This enables the work to be machined close to the zip.
    Further rows of machining may be added for decoration if wished.

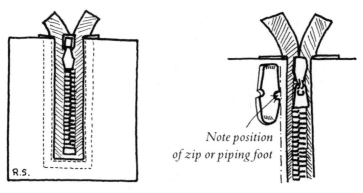

Note position of zip or piping foot

Zip machined in with zipper foot

Zip into a seam

This is perhaps the most used position for a zip. The edges of the seam may meet in the centre of the zip or one side of the seam may lap over the zip.

Seam Edges meeting in centre of Zip – very often used when the seam is at the centre front or centre back.

1. The seam is prepared for the whole length, but stitched only as far as the opening.
    The ends of the machining must be fastened off very securely.

The seam must be neatened, for the whole length, by a method suitable for the fabric.

Press the seam open, leaving the tacking stitches in.

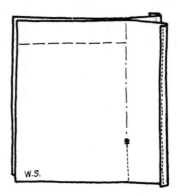

Zip opening unstitched

2. Place the right side of the zip to the wrong side of the garment and pin in position. The metal slide of the zip should lie just below the seam line of the top edge, and the teeth of the zip should lie exactly over the tacked portion of the seam. To do this it is best to fix only a small portion of the zip at a time.

   Tack the zip in position – the tacking stitches should go through to the right side of the garment.

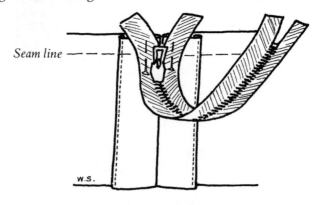

Placing zip in opening

3. From the right side, and using a zip foot, machine the zip into position.

Remove all tacking stitches including those over the teeth of the zip.

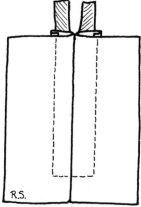

Machine on right side

4.   On the wrong side, the tapes of the zip should be hemmed to the seam turnings to stop them curling back during laundering and then catching in the teeth of the zip.

The ends of the tapes should also be hemmed to the seam turnings and for extra strength a piece of seam tape may be hemmed over the ends of the tape.

NB. None of these hemming stitches should show on the right side.

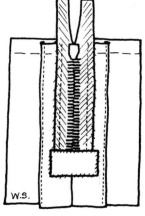

Neatening the zip

Lapped method – a good method for side seams

1.   The seam is made as far as the opening and neatened for the whole length (i.e. seam and opening) in a manner suitable for fabric.

2. The turning on the overwrap is folded to the wrong side on the seam line and tacked into position.
    The turning on the underwrap is folded back 2mm away from seam line and tacked into place.
    Press turnings very lightly.

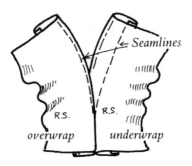

Folding the turnings in

3. The underwrap is fixed first.
    The closed zip is fixed right side uppermost with the slide of the zipper level with the top seam line and the teeth of the zip close to the tacked turning on underwrap. The tape of the zip lies under the underwrap.
    Pin and tack in position.
    Using a zip foot, machine the zip into position.
    Fasten ends of machining securely.
    Take out tacking stitches.

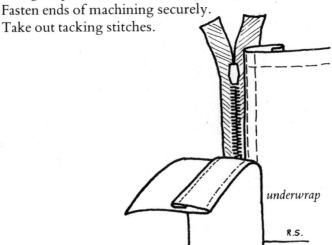

Zip stitched to underwrap turning

4. Lay the overwrap over the zip so that the tacked edge lies along the seam line on the underwrap. The first line of stitching should be concealed.

   Pin and tack the zip in position so that the stitches just clear the teeth of the zip (usually about 1cm away from fold).

   Using a zip foot, machine the zip into position.

   Fasten off ends of machining very securely.

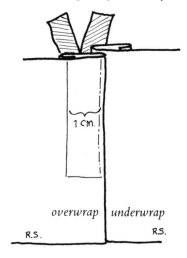

Zip machined to overwrap

5. The inside of the zip is finished as for centered method.

Zipped Fly Opening for Trousers

It is possible to buy in a limited range of colours, a special trouser zip which is slightly curved at the lower end. It is usual to incorporate a zip guard or fly flap in this method. This method is most often used on men's clothing and therefore the lap is left over right. If this method is used on women's clothes the lap may be reversed, if desired.

1. The crotch seam is stitched and neatened as far as the mark for the fly opening. The seam turnings are clipped and then pressed open.

2. **The zip guard and underwrap.** The turnings on the underwrap are folded to the wrong side 3mm beyond the seam line.

   Tack into position.

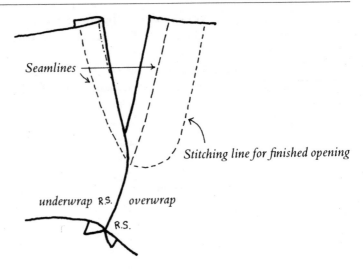

Seamlines

Stitching line for finished opening

underwrap R.S.   overwrap

R.S.

Turn in underwrap turnings

3.   The zip guard is made by placing the two right sides together.
Pin, tack and machine along the seam line allowances.
Trim and snip seam allowances.
Turn to right side and tack along the curved edge.
Baste through the middle of the zip guard.

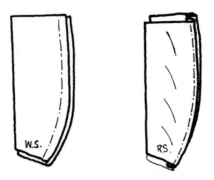

W.S.

R.S.

Making the zip guard

4.   The zip is positioned on wrong side of the underwrap so that the
slide is just below the seam line at top and the teeth of the zip are
close to the tacked edge of the underwrap.
Pin and tack into position.
Place the zip guard behind the zip so that the raw edges of the zip

guard are level with the seam turning on underwrap. Tack into position through all layers.

Use a zip foot and machine zip and zip guard to underlap and close to the folded edge.

On the wrong side the seam turning is zigzagged to the zip guard.

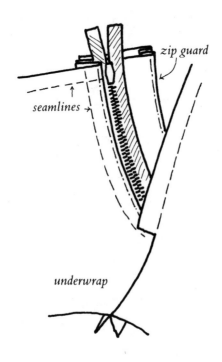

Positioning zip on underwrap

5. **The Overwrap**. The seam turning at the end of the opening on overwrap side is clipped so that the facing may be applied to the right side.

    Pin, tack and machine along the seam line.

    Seam allowance is trimmed and snipped.

    Turn facing to the wrong side of the overwrap.

    Work seam edge to top and tack into position. Press.

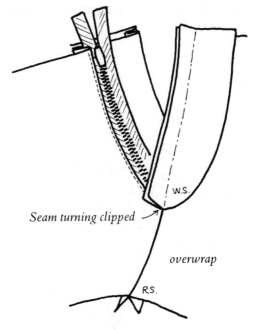

Seam turning clipped

overwrap

Facing on overwrap

6. The overwrap is lapped to its closed position. Baste along the length of the opening.

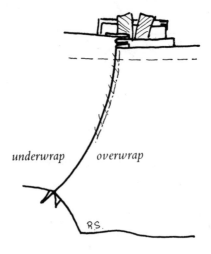

underwrap   *overwrap*

Overwrap basted in position

7. With the work flat, the zip guard is folded back and pinned to the wrong side of the underwrap.

   The overwrap is folded back from the facing so that the zip may be pinned, tacked and machined to the overwrap facing only.

   Fold back overwrap to flat position, but leave zip guard pinned back.

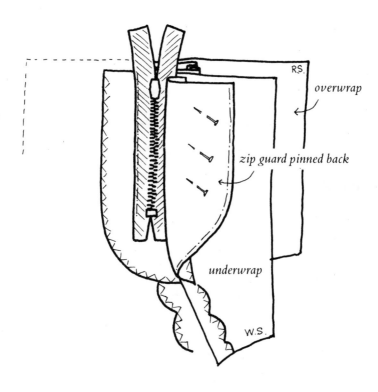

Zip stitched to overwrap facing

8. From the right side of work, machine facing to overwrap through the stitching line already marked on the overwrap. Finish in a small triangle at the base of the opening.

   On the inside, the ends of the zip tapes are finished in the usual way.

   Remove all tacking stitches and the pins holding zip guard back. Press.

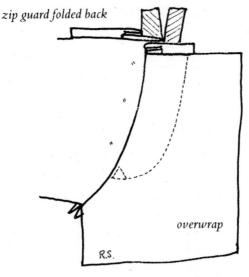

zip guard folded back

overwrap

R.S.

Trouser zip in position

Invisible Zip

When this type of zip is inserted correctly there is no stitching showing on the right side – the closed zip opening appears to be a continuation of the seam.

Instead of metal teeth that close together, each side of the zip consists of a nylon coil which interlocks when the zip slide goes over them.

A special zip foot is needed to sew this type of zip close to the coil.

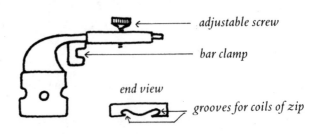

adjustable screw

bar clamp

end view

grooves for coils of zip

Special zip foot

1. Mark seam lines on sides of opening.
    The seam must NOT be sewn beforehand with this type of zip.

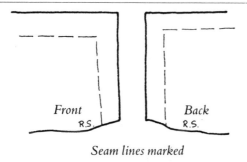

Seam lines marked

2. Place right side of the zip to the right side of the back so that the
    centre of the zip lies exactly on top of the seam line.
    The zip slide should be just below the seam line at top edge.
    Pin and tack the left hand zip tape into position.

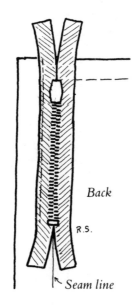

Zip placed on back seam line

3. Undo zip.
    Position special foot so that the right hand groove goes over the
    roll of the zip and the needle is in the centre position.
    Roll the coil to the right as the zip is machined in as far as the metal
    zip slide will allow, about 2cm from the bottom of the zip.

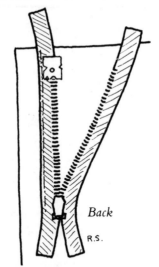

Showing position of zip foot

4. Close the zip and lay the right side of the zip to the seam
    line on the right side of the front seam.
    Tack into position.

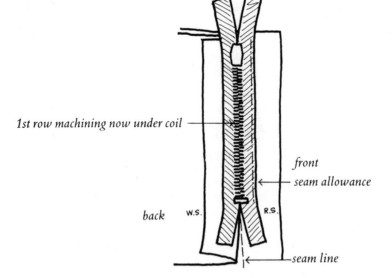

Tack zip to front of garment

5. Undo the zip.

Place the zip under the left hand groove of special zip foot with needle in centre position.

Roll the coil to the left as the zip is machined in (proceed as far as the metal zip slide allows).

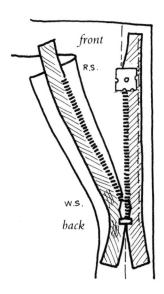

Machine second side while unzipped

6. The seam below the zip is now completed.

With the right sides together and seam lines matching, pin and tack along seam line below the zip.

The zip will need to be lifted out of the way to machine the seam.

Use zip foot with the needle position set to use the right hand side.

This will enable the seam machining to be joined accurately to the zip machining.

Fasten off ends of machining.

Neaten the seam edges according to the type of fabric.

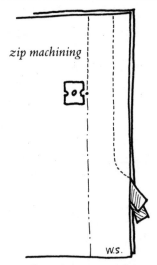

zip machining

W.S.

Complete seam and neaten

7.   The tapes of the zip are now machined to the seam turnings only
     for the complete length of the zip – first one side, refold, and then
     the other side.

     This will also sew the bottom 2cm of the zip which was not
     attached in the first instance.

     Seam tape is sewn across the ends of the zip tape in the usual way.

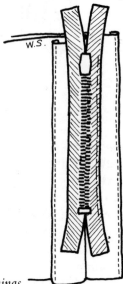

W.S.

Machine zip tapes to seam turnings

21

LININGS

1. The addition of a lining to a garment adds warmth.
2. Because a lining is usually silky to touch, a lined garment is made more comfortable to wear as, not only does the garment slip on more easily, but all turnings are concealed.
3. A lining helps to keep the garment in good shape and therefore to hang well.
4. The addition of a lining adds to the cost of the garment but this must be weighed against the extra wear obtained.

Materials for linings

1. The lining fabric must never be thicker than the fabric of the garment and usually it is thinner.
2. The colour of the lining is a personal choice, but usually the colour matches or tones. Sometimes a complete contrast is chosen, but it is unwise to choose a dark lining for a light fabric as this may alter the colour of the garment.
3. Linings should have a slippery surface to allow the garment to move easily in wear.
4. Lining fabric should be less expensive than garment fabric.

Materials suitable for lining are taffetas, satin, silk, smooth synthetic fibre crepes such as Tricel.

General Points for Linings

1. Generally linings are cut from the same pattern as the garment, but a 1.5cm pleat is allowed at the centre back to allow for movement.
2. The lining is thread marked in the usual way.

3.   The grain of the lining should match that of the garment – both warp and weft ways.
4.   If the style allows the side seams of the garment and lining are attached to one another.
5.   Lining hems are often left loose on full length garments, but attached at jacket hems.

To line a waistcoat to the edge of the garment

This is a useful method if the garment is required to be reversible.
1.   Baste interfacing to the wrong side of the front edge and neck and also to the wrong side of the back neck.
     Pin, tack and stitch darts in front and back.

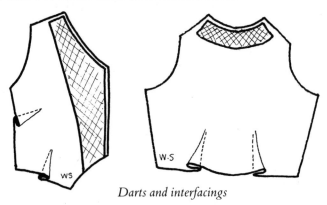

Darts and interfacings

2.   With the right sides facing, match balance points and seam lines on both shoulders. Pin, tack and machine. Remove the tacking stitches. Press the seam open.

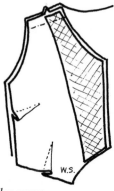

Join shoulder seams

3. Pin, tack and stitch the darts and shoulder seams on lining fabric. Press.

4. Place the right sides of waistcoat and lining together, matching shoulder seams, balance points and seam lines at armhole, neck and front edges. Pin and tack armhole edges on the seam line. Pin and tack neck, front and lower front edge as far as the dart (on the seamline). Machine. Remove the tacking stitches. Trim and layer the seam turnings; snip corners and curved edges.

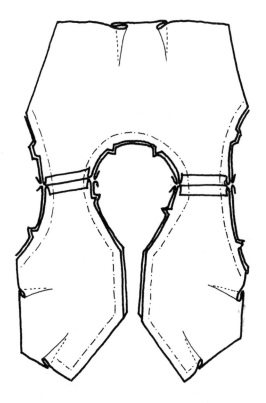

Match up with right sides together

5. Push the lower fronts beween the two layers of fabrics at the shoulder. Work the seams to the edges and tack into position.

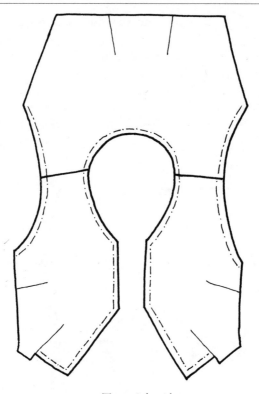

Turn right side out

6.   At the side seams with the right sides facing, match the front lining
     seam line to back lining seam line and front waistcoat seam line to
     back waistcoat seam line. The armhole seams should be exactly on
     top of one another. Pin, tack and machine the side seams. Press
     seams open.

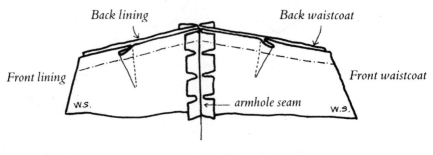

Side seams

7. Bring the waistcoat side seam and lining side seam together. Baste through seam.

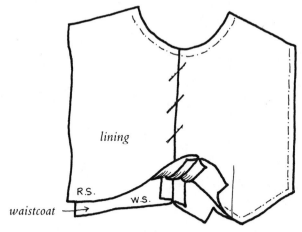

lining

R.S.

W.S.

waistcoat

Side seams together

8. At the lower edge, fold to the wrong side the turnings of the waistcoat and lining along their respective seam lines. Tack the two folds together. Slip stitch the two folds together. Remove tacking stitches. Press.

R.S.
lining

Join lower edges

To line a jacket with a faced front edge

1. The jacket should be completed as far as –
   Darts and seams stitched
   Front facing attached
   Collar attached
   Pockets (if any) completed.
2. The lining is completed as far as having the darts and seams stitched. Tack in the centre back pleat.
3. The sleeve seams in both the jacket and the lining are stitched, but

the sleeves are not set into the jacket.

4.   Pin the lining to the jacket at the centre back. Smooth lining to the sides and pin at least once on each side of centre back. Check that the grain lines are level. Baste into position.

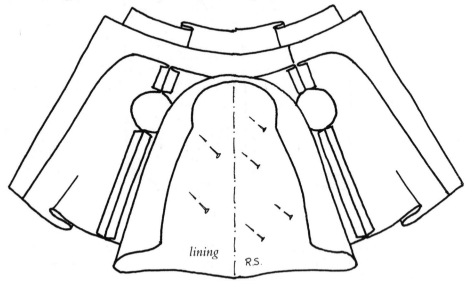

Lining pinned to jacket back

5.   Tack the lining side seams to the front seam allowance on the side seam of the jacket. Fold front lining towards the front.

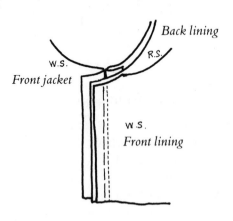

Side seams together

6. Pin front lining to front facing and back neck lining to back facing. Tack lining to jacket round the armhole.
7. Turn under the seam allowance at front, neck and hem of lining. Make sure the lining is very slightly fuller than the jacket so that there is no risk of the jacket being pulled out of shape. Tack lining into position. Hem the lining to the jacket all the way round, making sure that no stitches show through to the right side of the jacket.
8. Set the jacket sleeve into the armhole. Pin, tack and machine along seam line.
   Bring the jacket sleeve through to the inside of the jacket.

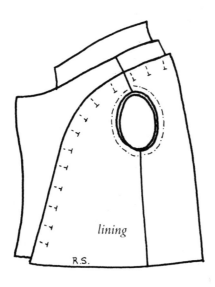

Lining pinned to facings

9. Slip sleeve lining over jacket sleeve and turn in seam allowance at the head of the sleeve. Hem the stitching at the armhole.
   Turn in hem allowance on sleeve lining and hem to hem on jacket sleeve.

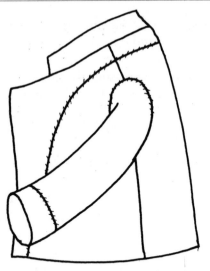

Linings hemmed in place

To line Skirts and Trousers

These should be lined before the waistband is set on, but with darts, seams and openings complete.

It is usual to leave the hem until the garment is lined and the waistband finished.

There are several ways of making trousers but if they are to be lined the most satisfactory method is the one which has the crotch seam done last. Complete 2 side seams and 2 inside leg seams, making sure a pair of legs is made.

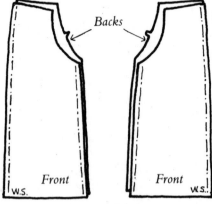

Trouser legs complete

Press seams open. Turn one leg to the right side and slip this leg inside the other leg. The crotch seam is tacked as far as the opening and then stitched on the seamline.

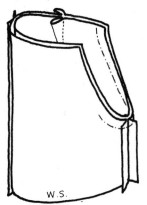

One leg inside the other

It is usual to put a second line of stitching very close to the first at the lowest part of the crotch seam.

The opening is then completed.

The lining is made in exactly the same way but the opening is not completed.

Drop the lining inside the skirt or trousers with the wrong sides facing.

For both skirts and trousers, at the opening, the seam allowance on the lining is turned in.

The lining is tacked into position round the opening (usually a zip) taking care to keep the lining away from the teeth of the zip.

Hem into position.

The waistband is then set on according to the style of the garment.

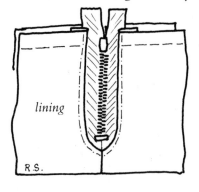

Lining tacked to top edge of skirt or trousers

Lining in position around opening

22

UNDERLINING

This should not be confused with interfacing as it serves a different purpose altogether.

Underlining is used when a loosely woven or transparent fabric needs extra body, e.g. loosely woven tweed needs underlining with holland or calico. Generally the whole of the garment is underlined before the garment is assembled.

Pattern pieces are cut out twice – once in the fabric and once in the underlining. It is very important to see that each piece of underlining has exactly the same grain as the section of garment to which it is being applied – this can only be done on a flat surface. The two pieces should be carefully basted together to form one piece of fabric and then the usual dressmaking processes are followed, including putting in interfacings where extra crispness is required.

23

PRESSING

A professional finish will not be obtained in dressmaking unless the work is pressed really well as the work progresses. It is a good maxim to remember, **'tack as you go, press as you sew'.**

1. Never press over pins.
2. Wherever possible avoid pressing over tacking stitches, as the imprint of the stitches may be left in the material. Where it is essential to press over tackings, press very lightly, remove the tackings and press again.
3. Always test the heat of the iron on a scrap of the material being pressed. The guide given on the iron thermostat is a rough guide as to what is needed. When the iron is too hot for the material being pressed, the material will scorch, melt, shrivel or harden.
4. Press the work on the wrong side wherever possible.
   If the work must be pressed on the right side, use a dry cloth between the garment and iron.
5. Pressing consists of placing the iron onto the portion of work to be pressed, holding there for a few seconds and lifting the iron to replace it a little further along. The iron is never slid along the material.
   Experience with different fabrics will indicate how hard to press each type of fabric to obtain a good result.

Dry Pressing – Suitable for cotton and cotton type fabrics.

This is pressing without any moisture and is suitable for many fabrics – particularly cottons and cotton type fabrics. Many of the latter are a mixture of fibres some of which are man-made and therefore care must be exercised with the heat of the iron.

Damp Pressing – Suitable for woollen and woollen type fabrics. Where an unsatisfactory result is obtained with dry pressing, damp pressing may be used. This may be done with a steam iron or by placing a damp muslin (not wringing wet) between the garment and the iron and pressing as for dry pressing. Any moisture left in the garment must be dispersed by dry pressing afterwards.

It must be remembered that moisture on the fabric may cause

    (a)   the fabric to shrink slightly

    (b)   water marks on the fabric

Therefore, always test on a scrap of same material before using this method.

Pressing Man-made Fibres

These can present quite a problem if one is not sure what fibres are contained in the fabric.

Always test on a scrap of the fabric in the following order.

    (a)   Dry press – gradually increasing the pressure and then temperature

    (b)   Damp press – gradually increasing the pressure then temperature

Pressing Pile and Brush Fabrics

These must be flattened as little as possible on the pile, but seams need to be pressed to obtain a professional result.

It is possible to buy a special velvet board on which to lay the pile surface of the fabric, but a thick turkish towel is a good substitute.

Press very lightly to begin with and increase pressure very gradually.

Special Points when pressing:

1. Seams

    (a)   Always press the turnings and stitching flat before pressing the seam open.

    (b)   To prevent the impression of seam turnings showing through to the right side, press seams on a covered roller.

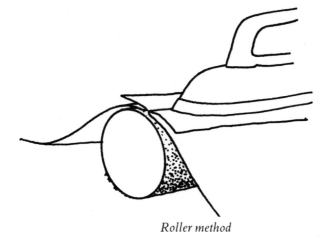

Roller method

OR Place brown paper between the seam turning and garment before pressing open.

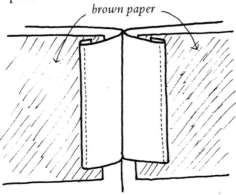

Brown paper method

2. **Darts**

    (a) Press the fold of the dart before pressing to one side either on a covered roller or on a tailors ham.

    (b) On thick materials, the fold of the dart should be cut and the dart pressed open.

3. **Pleats**

These are usually pressed very lightly on the wrong side with the tacking stitches left in.

Remove the tackings.

Cover with a damp muslin, press firmly with iron, remove iron and hold steam back in fabric with a wooden board. Dry press to thoroughly dry the fabric.

4. **Hems**

Care must be taken not to stretch any part of the hem which is on the bias.

Never press over the lower edge of the hem without putting brown paper or a piece of similar fabric close to the hem.

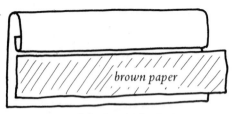

Pressing the hem

Shrinking Fullness away

This is usually only possible on woollen or woollen type fabrics. It is particularly useful to be able to do this at the head of a plain top sleeve or on a curved hem.

A fairly wet muslin is put over the part of the fabric to be shrunk on the wrong side and a fairly hot iron is held lightly over the muslin.

The steam will eventually shrink away unwanted fullness. The fabric should then be pressed dry with an iron at the correct temperature for the fabric.

Shiny Marks

These can be removed from woollen fabrics by using the method for shrinking but working on the right side of the fabric. Dry press the fabric on the wrong side to dry off.

The final press

If the garment has been well pressed during each stage of work the final press will be fairly quick and easy. All that should be required is that small creases in the fabric should be removed by ironing (as opposed to pressing) to freshen the fabric. Iron small parts of the garment before the main sections.

Hang on a hanger when finished.